Run Away from God?

James M. Boice

This book is designed for your personal reading pleasure and profit. It is also designed for group study. A leader's guide with helps and hints for teachers is available from your local Christian bookstore or from the publisher at $.75.

VICTOR BOOKS

a division of SP Publications, Inc., Wheaton, Illinois
Offices also in Fullerton, California • Whitby, Ontario, Canada • London, England

ACKNOWLEDGEMENTS

The author and editors are grateful for permission
to use quotations from the following books:
The Judgment of Jonah by Jacques Ellul, © 1971,
Wm. B. Eerdmans Publishing Co., Grand Rapids,
Michigan; Permission granted by the publisher.
You! Jonah! by Thomas John Carlisle, © 1968, Wm. B.
Eerdmans Publishing Co., Grand Rapids, Michigan;
Permission granted by the publisher.
Four Minor Prophets by Frank E. Gaebelein, © 1970,
Moody Press, Chicago, Illinois; Used by permission.
Born Again by Charles W. Colson, © 1976 by Charles
W. Colson; Published by Chosen Books, Inc., Used
by permission.

Scripture quotations in this book are from *The New
Scofield Reference Bible*, © 1967 by the Delegates of the
Oxford University Press, Inc., New York. Used by
permission.

Library of Congress Catalog Card Number: 77-75896
ISBN: 0-88207-501-2

© 1977, SP Publications, Inc. World rights reserved
Printed in the United States of America

VICTOR BOOKS
A division of SP Publications, Inc.
P. O. Box 1825 • Wheaton, Illinois 60187

TO GOD
gracious and merciful, slow to anger
and of great kindness

Contents

WHAT IF . . .

"Why me, Lord?"

© 1977 John V. Lawing, Jr. Used by permissi

Preface

Jonah is an historical character mentioned in 2 Kings 14:25, as well as in the Book of Jonah. But there is nothing remarkable in his mere existence. The importance of Jonah lies in his rebellion against God's command to him to preach to Nineveh and in God's subsequent dealings with him. In the course of the story much is taught about miracles, the mercy of God, and God's sovereignty in dealing with one whom He has commissioned but who runs away.

Still there is a sense in which any one of these items or even all together miss the point. For what we are really taught about in this short Old Testament story is ourselves—and about God in relationship to ourselves, since it is never possible to learn about one without learning about the other. In the synagogue on the Day of Atonement as part of the Jewish liturgy, this book is always read, and when the people have heard it they respond, "We are Jonah." True, we are all Jonah, Jews and Gentiles. That is the most important fact to be learned from a study of this book. We are Jonah in our disobedience, which sometimes is as extreme as his. We are Jonah in our frequent insensitivity to others. We are Jonah in our unhappiness at God's working even when we do obey Him. We are Jonah in our selfishness. In fact, there is not a point of the story in which we cannot see ourselves.

But we see God too, which is what makes this story bearable. We are disobedient, insensitive, unhappy with God, selfish (and more besides), but it is precisely with persons like this that God has to do. It is to people like this, like us, that He is gracious.

In this, as in all my writings, I am indebted to many both directly and indirectly. Most of the direct indebtedness is suggested in the quotations from the exceptional commentaries by Frank E. Gaebelein, Hugh Martin, and Jacques Ellul. The most important indirect indebtedness is to Donald Grey Barnhouse, one of my distinguished predecessors at Tenth Presbyterian Church in Philadelphia. He left no writing on Jonah, at least to my knowledge, but I have profited from his teaching through recordings. Some of his insights into Jonah show up in the first two of my chapters particularly.

I would like to acknowledge those places where I have given these messages verbally, in whole or in part, but the list has grown too long over the past few years for easy inclusion in a preface. As far as written versions go, a transcript of one of these series formed the basis for the messages on Jonah aired over the Bible Study Hour in January, 1977, and printed in the "Bible Studies" booklet for that month. The booklet is mailed to all supporters of the radio program. The only other printed material is an article entitled "Life With the Invisible Hand," which appeared in the November, 1976 issue of *Eternity* magazine.

It is my prayer that God will bless these studies to thousands of Christian people. He has already greatly blessed them to me.

Chapter 1

The Prophet
Who Ran Away

Many years ago in Chicago two homosexuals by the names of Leopold and Loeb were brought to trial for the murder of a young lad. Their lawyer was the well-known agnostic defense attorney Clarence Darrow, the man famous for his arguments at the Scopes trial regarding the teaching of evolution in the public schools of Tennessee. The Chicago trial was a long one, but at last it drew to a close and Darrow found himself summing up the evidence. The testimony of one witness had been particularly damaging. So Darrow referred to it saying, "Why, a person could as easily believe this man's testimony as he could believe that the whale swallowed Jonah."

Well, there were some people on the jury who believed that the whale had indeed swallowed Jonah. Moreover, they believed that Leopold and Loeb were guilty and so convicted them. But the sentence, "A person can as easily believe that as believe that the whale swallowed Jonah," became a rallying cry for those who wished to deny the truthfulness of this narrative.

Sign of Jonah

We live somewhat later in history and have knowledge about fish that was not available to those living in Darrow's day. We are less inclined to insist that the fish was a whale; neither the Old Testament Hebrew nor the New Testament Greek says "whale." The references are only to "a great fish." Nevertheless, those who adhere to the total trustworthiness of the Bible, now as then, rightly insist that Jonah was literally swallowed and was thus preserved alive for three days by the fish's action. To those who believe in the literal bodily resurrection of Jesus Christ, such an event is not at all impossible.

Moreover, there is a direct connection between the two. When unbelieving scribes and Pharisees asked Jesus for a sign that might substantiate His extraordinary claims, Jesus replied, "An evil and adulterous generation seeketh after a sign, and there shall no sign be given to it, but the sign of the prophet, Jonah; for as Jonah was three days and three nights in the belly of the great fish, so shall the Son of man be three days and three nights in the heart of the earth" (Matt. 12:39-40). In other words, Jesus referred to the experience of Jonah as an historical illustration of His own literal resurrection, thus reinforcing the truthfulness of this narrative. We stand with Him in this judgment.

To do so is not popular, of course. Nor will it gain the world's attention. If Christian people, and particularly a Christian minister, deny such things — if I should say, "Now, of course, a whale cannot swallow a man and therefore we know that we should not take the story of Jonah literally" — some people at least would pay attention. They would say, "Dr. Boice is denying the Bible. He does not believe in Jonah." This would be news. But if I maintain, as

I do, that this story is absolutely factual and, further-more, that the words of Christ also indicate that this is true, people shrug their shoulders and say, "Well, what do you expect a preacher to believe?" To re-gard Jonah as factual is not calculated to gain either respect or attention. Yet the book is true. Moreover, it is only when we actually regard it as true that it speaks to us fully.

There are a number of reasons why many will not believe the historical nature of Jonah's experience. They are summarized by Frank E. Gaebelein in *Four Minor Prophets* (Chicago: Moody Press, 1970, p. 60). He lists: (1) the abundance of the super-natural; (2) the unprecedented nature of Jonah's mission to Nineveh; (3) the reference to Nineveh in the past tense "was"; (4) the supposed grossly exag-gerated size of Nineveh; (5) supposed inaccuracies; and (6) the fact that the book contains late words supposedly incompatible with vocabulary used dur-ing the time Jonah was living.

But there are answers to each of these points, as Gaebelein shows (pp. 60-61). First, the problem with miracles simply begs the question of God's omnip-otence; for if God is able to raise up Jesus, He is certainly able to preserve Jonah and do the other supernatural acts attributed to Him. Second, other prophets also went to foreign nations—Elijah to Zarephath (1 Kings 17:8-24; Luke 4:26), Elisha to Damascus (2 Kings 8:7-15). Third, the use of "was" is merely a convention of narrative writing. Fourth, the reported size of Nineveh may well include the adjacent populations, what we would call suburbs. Fifth, the so-called inaccuracies are unproven. And sixth, so-called late words occur in Old Testament books from both early and late periods that are com-patible with the Book of Jonah.

Mercy and Sovereignty

There are other reasons beyond the miraculous to study this book. An obvious one is for what it teaches of the mercy of God. What is the story about if not God's mercy? There is the mercy of God to Nineveh, which made Jonah angry. There is the mercy of God to Jonah himself, for Jonah certainly did not deserve it. There is even the mercy of God to the pagan sailors mentioned in Jonah 1. These will be studied more fully in the next chapter. All these were recipients of God's mercy. If we understand the book at this point, we will find ourselves identifying with those who perhaps, from our natural point of view, are unworthy of such mercy. These will be people like the woman next door who lets her dog run through your flower bed, or like the couple down the street who are "swingers." They will be Jews or blacks, rich or poor, those of some other ethnic background, or someone who has wronged you by slander or a hostile act. These are the ones we should love for Christ's sake. As Gaebelein wrote: "In a day when prejudice and hate inflame men's emotions and pervert their judgment, Jonah speaks with compelling force about limiting our love and sympathies only to some of our fellow human beings and excluding others from our pity and compassion" (*Four Minor Prophets*, p. 125).

The Book of Jonah should also be studied for what it teaches about God's sovereignty, the point on which the book is most informative and the most profound. Understanding God's sovereignty is a problem for some Christians, though there are some features of sovereignty which are not a problem, of course. For example, most of us do not have problems with God's sovereign rule in natural law. Gravity is one illustration. God exercises His rule through gravity, and we do not have difficulty at this point. In fact, we are even somewhat reassured that objects conform to such laws.

The point at which we do have problems is when the sovereign will of God comes into opposition with a contrary human will. For example, there is the Christian who is married to another Christian but who, for whatever reason, is seeking a divorce. The Scriptures are plain. The couple are to remain together. But one declares, as a woman did to the author recently, "I know what the Bible says, but I don't care. I have had it. I am going to get a divorce anyway." What happens here?

Again, we may imagine a person who begins to get far from the Lord and who therefore gives up his or her times of Bible reading, fellowship with Christian friends, church attendance, and giving to support the Lord's work. Each of these duties is clearly prescribed in the pages of God's Word, but the Christian neglects them, sometimes with great energy and determination. What happens at that point? God could crush the human will and thereby accomplish His own purpose with a ruthless hand. There are times when He has done this, as in the contest between Moses and Pharaoh. But generally He does not. What happens in such cases? Does God give up? Does He change His mind? Or does He accomplish His purposes in some other way, perhaps indirectly? The answer is in the Book of Jonah.

A Great Commission

Interestingly enough, the book starts with a lesson on sovereignty—a commission to Jonah, and with Jonah's refusal to heed it. In other words, it begins with a formal expression of God's sovereign will and with a man's determined opposition to it. We read,

"Now the word of the Lord came unto Jonah, the son of Amittai, saying, 'Arise, go to Nineveh, that great city, and cry against it; for their wickedness is come up before me.' But Jonah rose up to flee unto Tarshish from the presence of the Lord" (1:1-3).

The location of Tarshish is often disputed. It has been identified with one of the cities of Phoenicia, but this is unlikely. It has been identified with ancient Carthage. Most probably, Tarshish was on the far coast of Spain, beyond Gibraltar. And if this was true, it means that in his disobedience Jonah was determined to go as far as possible in the opposite direction from where God was sending him. Nineveh was east. Tarshish was west. We can visualize the geography if we imagine Jonah coming out of his house in Palestine, looking left down the long road that led around the great Arabian desert to the valleys of the Tigris and Euphrates Rivers, and then turning on his heel and going down the road to his right.

Why did he do it? We can imagine some possible reasons. We can image, first, that Jonah was overcome by thoughts of the mission's *difficulties*, which are expressed very well in the commission which God Himself gave Jonah. God told Jonah that Nineveh was a very "great city," and indeed it was. In addition to what the book itself tells us—that the city was so large that it took three days to cross it and that it had 120,000 infants or small children (4:11)—we also know that it was the capital of the great Assyrian empire, that it had walls a hundred feet high and so broad that three chariots could run abreast around them. Within the walls were gardens and even fields for cattle. For a man to arrive all alone with a message from an unknown God against such a city was ludicrous in the extreme. What could one man do? Who would listen? Where were the armies that could break down such walls or storm such garrisons? The men of Nineveh would ridicule the strange Jewish prophet. "Certainly," as Hugh Martin, one of the most comprehensive commentators on this book, has written, "Jonah could not but foresee that some such reception in 'that great city' was about the most friendly he could anticipate. To be despised and simply laughed at, as a fanatic and fool, must have appeared to him inevitable, if indeed his fate should not be worse."[1] If Jonah had been overcome with the thought of the difficulties of such a mission and because of them had fled to Tarshish, we could well understand him. Yet not a word in the story indicates that it was the difficulties that upset this rebellious prophet.

Perhaps it was *danger*? The second word in God's description of the city is "wickedness." If Jonah had taken note of that wickedness and had refused to obey for that reason, this too would be understandable. Indeed, the more we learn of Nineveh the more dangerous the mission becomes. We think of the prophecy of Nahum, for example. Nahum's entire prophecy was against the wickedness of Nineveh, and the descriptions of it are vivid. "Woe to the bloody city! It is all full of lies and robbery; the prey departeth not; the noise of a whip, and the noise of the rattling of the wheels, and of the prancing horses, and of the bounding chariots. The horseman lifteth up both the bright sword and the glittering spear; and there is a multitude of slain, and a great number of carcasses; and there is no end of their corpses; they stumble upon their corpses, because

[1]Hugh Martin, *The Prophet Jonah: His Character and Mission to Nineveh*, original edition, 1866 (London: Banner of Truth Trust, 1958), p. 40.

of the multitude of the harlotries of the well-favored harlot, the mistress of witchcrafts, that selleth nations through her harlotries, and families through her witchcrafts. 'Behold, I am against thee,' saith the Lord of hosts, 'and I will uncover thy skirts from thy face, and I will show the nations thy nakedness, and the kingdoms thy shame'" (Nahum 3:1-5).

What was one poor preacher to do against such pride and hardness? Indeed, would they not simply kill him and add his body to the already high heap of carcasses? Thoughts like these could have made Jonah afraid; and if he had been afraid, we would not blame him. But again, not a word in the story indicates that it was danger that turned Jonah in the opposite direction.

What was the reason then? In the fourth chapter of the book, after God had already brought about the revival and had spared the Ninevites from judgment, Jonah explained the reason, arguing that it was precisely because of this outcome that he had disobeyed originally. That is, he declared that he knew God was gracious and that God was not sending him to Nineveh only to announce a pending judgment, but rather that Nineveh might repent. Jonah's own words are: "O Lord, was not this my saying, when I was yet in my country? Therefore, I fled before unto Tarshish; for I knew that Thou art a gracious God, and merciful, slow to anger, and of great kindness, and repentest Thee of the evil" (4:2).

As we read these words carefully we realize the reason why Jonah did not want to go to Nineveh. Those who lived there were the enemies of his people, the Jews, and he was afraid that if he did go to them with his message of judgment, they would believe it and repent, and God would bless them. And he did not want them blessed! God could bless

Israel. But Jonah would be damned (literally) before he would see God's blessing shed upon these enemies. So he fled to Tarshish. We can understand the geography involved and Jonah's motives if we can imagine the word of the Lord coming to a Jew who lived in New York during World War II, telling him to go to Berlin to preach to Nazi Germany. Instead of this, he goes to San Francisco and there takes a boat for Hong Kong.

We may laugh at that, of course. But before we laugh too hard we should ask whether or not we are in the spiritual ancestry of Jonah. True, we have never been sent to Nineveh, and we may never have to run away to Tarshish. But the commission that has been given to us is no less demanding than Jonah's, if we are Christians. And often our attempts to avoid it are no less determined than were Jonah's, when he tried to run away.

Most Christian people come into contact with the world in at least three places: in their neighborhoods, at work (unless they work for a totally Christian organization), and in their spare-time activities—their clubs, hobbies, sports, and adult education courses. The people they meet in these places all have great needs. They need to know Christ, first of all, if they are not Christians. But they also need friendship, understanding, achievement. In some cases, there are even physical needs brought on by sickness, poverty, or some other physical privation. But Christians are often strangely insensitive to these needs and make excuses in order to avoid the personal sacrifices necessary to carry out the work of Christ. They say—we have all heard the excuses and, I am afraid, often make them ourselves—"I am too busy," "I have too many problems of my own," "Charity begins at home," or even "I am not called."

Jonah's commission consisted of three main words. He was told to "arise." He was told to "go." He was told to "cry" — precisely what we have been told to do in the Great Commission. We are to arise from wherever we happen to be seated. We are to go into all the world. And we are to cry against the world's wickedness, teaching it all that we have been taught by Jesus. Matthew's form of the Great Commission says, "Go ye, therefore, and teach all nations, baptizing them in the name of the Father, and of the Son, and of the Holy Spirit, teaching them to observe all things whatsoever I have commanded you; and, lo, I am with you always, even unto the end of the age" (Matt. 28:19-20). We are to arise; but sometimes we remain seated, often in the pews of our churches where the world seldom comes. We are to go; but we remain inactive. We are to cry; but generally our tongues are strangely silent.

Strangely silent! Strange that we should be silent when there is such a wonderful story to tell! John R. W. Stott illustrated what we often do in his book *Our Guilty Silence* (Chicago: InterVarsity Press, 1967, pp. 9-10). He described how he was on an overnight train from London to Pembrokeshire in South Wales and how a young land agent, who shared the sleeper, repeatedly took the name of the Lord Jesus Christ in vain. He had the upper bunk. In the morning, while getting ready to wash, he accidentally dropped his shaving equipment and swore about it. At this point Stott remained silent, making all the usual excuses — "It's none of your business," "You've no responsibility for him," "He'll only laugh at you." It was only after an inner struggle of some 15 minutes that he eventually spoke of Christ and managed to leave the man an evangelistic booklet. We all have these difficulties. Only not all of us eventually overcome them and actually share the Gospel.

✓ Wings of the Morning

Verse 3 tells us of Jonah's attempt to get away from God, and gives us the consequences of that attempt. It is surprising that Jonah did not know of these consequences before he ran or consider how impossible it was to escape God.

Jonah lived relatively late in Old Testament history, certainly long after the psalms were written; he therefore had ample opportunity to know those great words in Psalm 139: "Whither shall I go from Thy Spirit? Or whither shall I flee from Thy presence? If I ascend up into heaven, Thou art there; if I make my bed in Sheol, behold, Thou art there. If I take the wings of the morning, and dwell in the uttermost parts of the sea, even there shall Thy hand lead me, and Thy right hand shall hold me" (vv. 7-10). Did Jonah know these words? Probably. Then why did he not remember them as he set out in the ship for Tarshish?

As I read that psalm I find myself wondering if the name of the ship upon which Jonah set out might not have been *The Wings of the Morning*. The story does not give the name. But that would have been a good name for a ship; and if the ship mentioned in the Book of Jonah were so named, how well suited it would have been to Jonah's situation! Did he notice the name, if this is what it was? Did he notice the rats getting off as he stepped on? If I understand sin and disobedience at all, I suspect that Jonah noticed none of these things, so set was he in his folly. No more do we when we take our "wings of the morning"—whether they be a preoccupation with a job, an attitude, a cherished sin, or some other form of disobedience — to sail away from God across life's sea.

God's Sovereignty

At this point we find our first great lesson regarding God's sovereignty. Built into Jonah's first attempts to get away from God are two results which will inevitably follow anyone who tries to disobey Him. These results, which are mentioned in verse 3, come one verse before the mention of God's sending the storm after Jonah's ship. God has His special interventions too, but the fact that the results appear before God's interventions indicates that they are as inevitable in spiritual matters as are physical laws in the natural universe.

The first result is that Jonah's course was downhill. He would not have described it that way. He would have said that he was improving his lot in life, just as we also do when we choose our own course instead of God's. But it was downhill nevertheless. In verse 3, we are told that Jonah went "down" to Joppa and that having paid his fare he went "down" into the ship. This is not accidental in a story in which the words are as carefully chosen as in this one. Nor are these two instances of the word "down" isolated. Two verses farther on, in verse 5, we are told that Jonah had gone "down" into the sides of the ship, that is, below decks. Then in chapter 2, verse 6, in a prayer which takes place after Jonah has been thrown overboard by the sailors, Jonah describes how he had gone "down" to the bottom of the earth's mountains beneath the waves. That is a lot of going down! Down, down, down, down. But it is always that way when a person runs from the presence of the Lord. The way of the Lord is up! Consequently, any way that is away from Him is down. The way may look beautiful when we start.

The seas may look peaceful and the ship attractive, but the way is still down.

There was another result. In his excellent preaching on Jonah, Donald Grey Barnhouse often called attention to it by highlighting the phrase "he paid his fare." He noted that Jonah did not get to where he was going, since he was thrown overboard, and that he obviously did not get a refund on his ticket. So he paid the full fare and did not get to the end of his journey. Barnhouse said, "It is always that way. When you run away from the Lord you never get to where you are going, and you always pay your own fare. On the other hand, when you go the Lord's way you always get to where you are going, and He pays the fare." That is worth repeating: *When you run away from the Lord you never get to where you are going, and you always pay your own fare. But when you go the Lord's way you always get to where you are going, and He pays the fare.*

The Book of Jonah illustrates one half of that statement. The story of Moses' mother, Jochebed, illustrates the other half. Jochebed conceived Moses during a time of great persecution by the Egyptians, a time in which Hebrew male infants were being thrown into the river to die. When the child was born, Jochebed and her husband, Amram, tried to hide him as long as possible, suspecting, I believe, that this was the one who had been promised by God to be the deliverer of the people. But at last the baby's cries grew too loud, and another plan was necessary. The mother made a little boat of bulrushes, covering it with tar. She placed Moses in it and set it in the reeds by the riverbank. Then she stationed Miriam, Moses' sister, at a distance to see what would become of him. Though she wanted her baby more than anything else in the world, Jochebed entrusted the matter to God, allowing Him to do as He wished with her and the child.

The daughter of Pharaoh came down to the river, saw the ark in the water, and sent her maids to fetch it. When it was opened, she saw the baby. He was crying. This so touched the woman's heart that she determined to save him and raise him in the palace. But what was she to do? Obviously the child needed a wet nurse. Where could she find one?

At this point, Miriam, who had been watching from a distance, came forward and asked if she could be of assistance. "Shall I go and call to thee a nurse of the Hebrew women, that she may nurse the child for thee?" Miriam asked.

"Yes," said the princess. So Jochebed was brought.

Jochebed was about to receive back the child she most dearly wanted. She would have done anything to have kept him. She would have scrubbed floors in the palace! In fact, if the daughter of the Pharaoh had said, "I am going to give you this child to raise. But I want you to know that I have seen through your stratagem. I know that this young girl was not up on that hill watching by accident. She must be the sister of this baby and, therefore, you must be the mother. You can have your child. But as a sign of your disobedience to the Pharaoh, I am going to cut off your right hand"...if she had said that, Moses' mother would probably have held out both hands, if only she could have had the child back. But that is not what happened. Instead, Pharaoh's daughter gave the child back, declaring, "Take this child away, and nurse it for me, *and I will give thee thy wages*" (Ex. 2:9, Italics mine).

"I will give thee thy wages." That is the point for which I tell the story. Jonah went his own way, paid his own fare, and got nothing. Jochebed went God's way. Consequently, God paid the fare, and she got everything. So I repeat it once more: When you run away from the Lord you never get to where you are going, and you always pay your own fare. But when you go the Lord's way you always get to where you are going, and He pays the fare.

But the Lord

In one sense Jonah's story is over at this point; that is, the story of his choice, his disobedience, is over. God has given His command. Jonah has disobeyed. Now Jonah must sit back and suffer the consequences as God intervenes supernaturally to alter the story. This is made very clear by the contrast between the first two words of verse 3 ("But Jonah") and the first three words of verse 4 ("But the Lord"). It is true that Jonah has rejected God. He has voiced his little "but," as we sometimes do. He is allowed to do it. God's sovereignty does not rule it out. But now God is about to voice His "but," and His is more substantial than Jonah's.

What did God do? He did three *great* things. First, He sent a _great storm_. The text indicates that it was a storm of unusual ferocity, so fierce that even experienced sailors were frightened. Each time I read about it I think of that other storm that also frightened experienced men on the Sea of Galilee. The men were Christ's disciples, and Christ was with them, though asleep in the boat. For awhile they rowed. But they were in danger of sinking and were afraid. So they awoke Jesus and cried, "Lord, save us; we perish."

Jesus replied, "Why are ye fearful, O ye of little faith?" Then He arose, and rebuked the winds and the sea; and there was a great calm. But the [disciples] marveled, saying, 'What manner of man

is this, that even the winds and the sea obey Him?'"
(Matt. 8:23-27)

Note the contrast. The Lord who can calm the
troubled waters of your life is the same Lord who can
stir them up to great frenzy. What He does depends
on whether He is with you in the boat or, a better
way of putting it, whether or not you are with Him.
If Jesus is in your boat—if you are going His way and
are trusting Him—then, when the storms come, you
can cry out, "Oh, Master, help me!" and He will
calm the violence. But if you are running from Him—
if He is not in your boat and you are disobeying
Him—then He will stir the waves up.

Second, the Lord prepared a *great fish*. Farther
on in the story God also prepared a small worm to
eat the root and so destroy the plant that shaded
Jonah. On the one hand, God used one of the largest
creatures on earth to do His bidding. On the other
hand, He used one of the smallest. Apparently it
makes no difference to God. He will use whatever
it takes to get the disobedient one back into the
place of blessing. Are you running away from God?
If so, He may use the cankerworm to spoil your har-
vest. He may use the whirlwind to destroy your barns
and buildings. If necessary, He will touch your person. He will use whatever it takes, because He is
faithful to Himself, to you, and to His purposes.

Finally, God saved a *great city*. This last act, like
the others, is an act of mercy. For the city did not
deserve His mercy. Yet He saved it, thereby preserv-
ing it from destruction for a time.

A Continuous Performance

God's perseverance will be discussed in later chapters, but it is helpful to look at it in anticipation even
now. To summarize the principles in these opening

verses there is a great verse on perseverance from the Apostle Paul's writings: "Being confident of this very thing, that He who hath begun a good work in you will [keep on performing] it until the day of Jesus Christ" (Phil. 1:6).

Quite often we look at that verse merely as a statement of the "eternal security" of the Christian, which is right. God will certainly continue His work with us, regardless of what happens, and will preserve us for heaven. But this verse also means—we must not miss it—that God is so determined to perfect His good work in us that He will continue to do so with whatever it takes, regardless of the obedience or disobedience of the Christian. Will you go in His way? Then He will bless your life and encourage you. Will you run, as Jonah ran? Then He will trouble your life. If necessary, He will even break it into little pieces, if by so doing He enables you to walk in His way once again. If you disobey, you will find your initial disobedience easy. But after that the way will grow hard. On the other hand, if you obey Him, you will find the way smoothed out and filled with blessing.

Chapter 2

The God Who Will Not Let Go

The lessons of the first three verses of Jonah are great, for they concern the impossibility of running away from God and the consequences of such an attempt. The consequences are that the path we take is always downhill, that we never get to where we are going, and that we always pay our own bills. At this point of the story, however, God Himself intervened in a supernatural way, so that the lessons of the remainder of the chapter are just as great as those at the beginning. In particular, we learn that this disobedience of one of God's servants always involves others in his peril. We also learn how God acts when His will is opposed.

Special Intervention

The way God operates when His will is opposed by human beings leads again to the issue of God's sovereignty and carries us a step farther in our understanding of it. First we saw that God's sovereignty expresses itself in what we might call a natural spiritual order. According to this principle, no path of disobedience is ever blessed. But now we also learn that God will intervene in special ways to insure the accomplishment of His purposes.

This special intervention occurs twice in the first chapter. The first is in the way God dealt with Jonah when he ran away.

The second is in God's dealing with the mariners. Jonah had sinned. According to some theologies, in which almost everything depends upon man's obedience to God and very little upon God's elective purposes with man, this should have been the end of the matter. If Jonah had sinned, God should simply have said, "Jonah, you have done it now. You have disobeyed Me, and as a result of that you have forfeited the right to be called My child. I am casting you off." That kind of response makes sense according to a man-centered theology or to any wisdom that we may have. But it is not the way God operates. To put it in theological language, God had elected Jonah to a special task, and He had determined that the task be accomplished. In other words, God took His election of Jonah so seriously that He would actually sink the ship on which the disobedient prophet was riding, if necessary, rather than allow him to get on to his own destination. The story says, "But the Lord sent out a great wind into the sea, and there was a mighty tempest in the sea, so that the ship was in danger of being broken" (v. 4).

One verse earlier we read the words "but Jonah." That verse tells us of Jonah's act of disobedience. We might say that those two words, "but Jonah," represent human depravity expressing itself through the old nature. In verse 4, in place of the words "but Jonah," we have the words "but the Lord." "But the Lord" is an expression of the sovereign grace of God persevering with His people.

There is no question about our ability to resist God or disobey Him. We all do it, and we do it easily. Though a pagan, Virgil wrote correctly, *"Facilis decensus Averno"* ("The descent to hell is easy"). When we disobey Him, God does not rearrange the stars of heaven to say, "Stop, do not go farther." He lets us go. At first He does not put great obstacles in our path. If we choose to stop reading our Bibles, He does not send a special prophet to get us reading them again. If we stop praying, He does not send a disaster into our lives to make us turn to Him. Not at first! He simply allows us to go downhill and to pay for our own foolish choices. However, when we persist in our disobedience, He gets rougher. He begins gently, just as we gently disobey. But in the end He sends the tempest.

What is the outcome of the great storm? Simply that by means of it God accomplished His purposes with Jonah. He accomplished His purposes with the people of Nineveh. He even accomplished His purposes in an ironic and preparatory way with the unbelieving sailors, for they came to believe on Him, as the story indicates.

The Mariners

The disobedience of one of God's servants always involves others in peril, even innocent people. For Achan's sin, all Israel was defeated at Ai. For the sin of David in numbering the people, 70,000 died of pestilence. Similarly, because of Jonah's sin, innocent mariners were on the verge of drowning. They knew how to sail a ship, but this storm was beyond them. So we are told that they were "afraid" of it and "cried every man unto his god, and cast forth the wares that were in the ship into the sea, to lighten it of them" (v. 5).

The mariners were like today's world's leaders who, though they are not godly men, nevertheless do as well as they know how to do to cope with the world's problems. I admire the mariners. As I read the story I find them to be hard-working, courageous men who know their business well. These men had been in storms before. They knew what to do. They knew that in great storms the solution was to lighten the ship by casting the wares overboard, which they did. Nevertheless, the storm was go great it frightened them, even though they did all they could to save the situation. When they could do nothing more, they called upon their gods.

Is this not a picture of today's world? Is it not a picture of government and politics? The trouble with the world's leaders is not that they are incompetent men. It is rather that the problems they are attempting to tackle are just too big for them. I am glad I do not have to deal with the world's sagging economy today. I am glad I don't have to struggle to eliminate misunderstanding between nations in order to advance world peace. These enormous problems are quite beyond any human ability, regardless of how talented the statesman. So we see such men trying everything possible and then, when all else fails, calling on God.

This is how we can tell that a political speech is drawing to a close. The typical political speech has three parts. First, there is the description of how bad things are and why no one else is able to solve the problems (if the politician is not in office), or else all that has been done to solve them (if the politician is in office). Second, there is the explanation of why the person speaking is the only one able to deal with what lies ahead. Third, an appeal is made to God for help. But the third part lasts only a few seconds. So when the appeal to God is made we know that 28 minutes of air time has expired and there will soon be a commercial break.

But we must not be smug at this point and overly blame the mariners, for we remember that the trouble that came upon them had come because of Jonah. And this means that, in some situations at least, problems come upon the world because of God's judgment upon His own children.

The brilliant French writer Jacques Ellul has a wonderful paragraph in which he shows how inseparably the lives of Christians and non-Christians are linked in this world. He writes, "The safety of all depends on what each does. But each has his own thing to do. They are in the same storm, subject to the same peril, and they want the same outcome. They are in a unique enterprise, and this ship typifies our situation. What do these sailors do? First, they do all they humanly can; while Jonah sleeps, they try all human methods to save the vessel, to keep the enterprise going (v. 5). What experience, nautical science, reason, and common sense teach them to do, they do. In this sense they do their duty. The sailors are in charge of the world, and in normal conditions they discharge their task correctly. We can ask no more of them. The tragic thing here, however, is that if conditions cease to be normal, it is not the fault of the sailors, the pagans; it is the fault of the Christian who has sailed with them. It is because of him that the situation is such that the knowledge and tradition of the sailors can do no more." Ellul continues, "We have to realize once again that this is how it usually is with the world; the storm is unleashed because of the unfaithfulness of the Church and Christians. This being so, if the tempest is God's will to constrain His Church, a will by which the whole human enterprise is endangered, one can easily see why man's technical devices are of no avail" (*The Judgement of Jonah*, Grand Rapids: Eerdmans, 1971, p. 41).

Note that while the storm was raging, Jonah, who represents the Church, was asleep deep within the sides of the ship. How many of God's people are asleep today? How many are impervious while the tempest rages?

You Can't Sleep Forever

When Jonah had gone down into the sides of the ship to sleep, seemingly in drugged indifference to the calling of God, he must have thought himself alone and safe, at least for the time being. But suddenly his sleep was interrupted by the "chief pilot," as the Hebrew word translated "shipmaster" in the King James Version means. This man was a pagan, like the others. He did not know the true God. His ideas of religion were undoubtedly filled with superstitions. Nevertheless, he believed enough in united, prevailing prayer to want all on board to pray together. Since he did not know Jonah or what god he worshiped, it was just possible that Jonah worshiped a god who could do something if the other gods failed.

His words were abrupt, for he was disturbed that Jonah could sleep when the ship was in such peril. "What meanest thou, O sleeper? Arise, call upon thy God, if so be that God will think upon us, that we perish not" (v. 6). Even a Christian is not allowed to ignore reality forever.

Meanwhile, up on the deck of the ship, the mariners had been discussing the storm and had concluded that it was not at all like other storms they had witnessed. They had been able to handle other storms. But this storm was ferocious, supernatural. Verse 4, which tells how "the Lord sent out a great wind into the sea," literally says that the Lord "hurled" the tempest. The mariners had concluded that the storm was a judgment against one of their number who had done something horrible. So they decided to cast lots to discover the culprit. It was at this moment that Jonah arrived from below deck.

Nothing in life ever really happens by chance. So when the lot was cast, the lot inevitably singled out Jonah.

People may think that such things are determined by chance. They speak of "Lady Luck" or work out "mathematical" odds. But God tells us that when the outcome really matters, and at other times too, He controls what happens. A verse in Proverbs says: "The lot is cast into the lap, but the whole disposing thereof is of the Lord" (Prov. 16:33). In this case the lot was something like a pair of dice, made from the anklebone of a sheep; the lap was the flat surface made when a man, who in those days normally wore a long garment, would squat down and spread his knees. So the dice were cast into the lap, and God determined the outcome. Donald Grey Barnhouse often paraphrased this verse by saying that "man throws the dice; but it is God who makes the spots come up."

Many Questions

As soon as Jonah was singled out by lot, a flurry of questions came pouring forth from the troubled mariners. This would have happened in any case, but it was especially true of Jonah in that no one really knew him. We catch some of the flavor of this from the writing. "Then said they unto him, 'Tell us, we pray thee, for whose cause this evil is upon us. What is thine occupation? And from where comest thou? What is thy country? And of what people art thou?'" (v. 8) Undoubtedly there were more questions even than these. Every man would have one. But at last they were all out. Then Jonah had his turn to speak. Every eye was on him.

Notice the irony of this situation. Jonah had run away from God and was in this difficult position simply because he would not preach to pagans. But here he was, in spite of himself, about to do precisely that. It is even possible that there were men of Nineveh among these sailors. God was about to show that His purposes will always be accomplished, even (if He so wills it) by one who is obstinately disobedient.

It is amusing to me that, in spite of his determination to disobey God and the rupture of fellowship between himself and God which that must have caused, Jonah gave a very good testimony. Perhaps he had been a preacher too long, and the habit of it was with him. Or perhaps, like Peter at the campfire of the high priest, he was just unable to lie convincingly. Logically, he might have been able to tell just the bare facts and let it go at that. Verse 10 tells that he did rehearse his entire story, culminating in his running away. But Jonah could not stop at that point, it seems. So even in his state of disobedience and in the trauma of the moment, Jonah told of his background and indicated that he was a servant of the Creator and covenant-keeping God, Jehovah. Moreover, he was brilliantly relevant as he said it. For he said, "I am an Hebrew; and I fear the Lord, the God of heaven, who hath made the sea [they needed a god who made the sea just then] and the dry land [the very place where each of them most wanted to be]" (v. 9).

Gaebelein writes of this testimony, "In addition to acknowledging himself a Hebrew, [Jonah] gave a witness then and there for his Lord. He may have been endeavoring to resign his commission, but he could not change his heart, which remained that of a true prophet. So he pointed these mariners to the only Lord God." (*Four Minor Prophets*, p. 78).

An interesting phrase appears here. For having been told of Jonah's testimony, we are immediately informed, "Then were the men exceedingly afraid." We have already been told once that the men were afraid; they were afraid of the storm. We will be told once more that as a result of God's act in calming it they "feared [that is, reverenced] the Lord exceedingly" (v. 16). But why, we might ask, were the men *exceedingly* afraid, at this point, more afraid apparently than they were of the storm itself?

The reason was that they knew about Jonah's God. These were mariners. They had undoubtedly traveled from port to port around the Mediterranean Sea, hearing many stories of other people and their gods. Are we to think that they had never heard of the Hebrew people or of the Hebrew God, Jehovah? Of course, they had heard of Him. He was the God who had brought down the plagues upon the Egyptians so that His people might be led out of Egypt. This was the God who had parted the waters of the Red Sea to allow the Jews to escape into the desert and who had then closed the waters on the pursuing Egyptian forces. This God had led the Hebrews in the wilderness for 40 years, protecting them by a cloud which spread out over their encampment during the daytime to give them shade but which turned into a pillar of fire by night to give them light and heat. He had provided manna to eat and water to drink. He had parted the waters of the Jordan River to enable them to cross over into Canaan. He had leveled the walls of Jericho. He had caused the sun to stand still at Gibeon so that Joshua would have time to achieve a full victory over the fleeing Amorites. This was the great God of the Hebrews; and it was this God, not a weak god, who was pursuing them for the sake of Jonah.

No wonder the men feared exceedingly. "Why hast thou done this?" they asked. "What shall we do for thee, that the sea may be calm unto us?" was their next and inevitable question (vv. 10-11).

Two More Questions

It is too bad that Jonah did not learn as much from the question the mariners first asked him as they had from his testimony, or he would not have answered the second question so poorly.

The mariners had asked, "Why has thou done this?" It was a rebuke. If Jonah had answered it properly, it would probably have led to his repentance. For there was no answer to it but the full confession of sin. Martin deals well with this question. "Suppose yourself in Jonah's place," he writes, "and hear the question put to you—to you, a man of God, by heathen men, 'Why hast thou done this?' Did your God provoke you to flee from Him? Did He deal so hardly and unkindly with you that you had no alternative but flight? Were you so tired of your God? Had you found Him out—as no more worthy of your trust and obedience? Had you got to the end of all the duty that you owed to Him—or of all the protection and support that He could afford to you? Why didn't you listen to Him?

"Produce your strong reasons. Has God been a wilderness to you? Have you found a better friend? Have you found a worthier portion? Have you found a sweeter employment than meditation in His word and calling on His name? . . .

"Have you found Him unfaithful to His promise? Have you discovered that He discourages His people? Will you say that the more you have known Him, the less you have thought of Him? It looks like it, O backslider. It looks like it, if you can remember days when you loved Him more, and served Him better than now" (*The Prophet Jonah*, p. 167-168). If Jonah had been able to think clearly along these lines, he would have acknowledged that nothing God had done or could ever do could deserve his disobedience; and he might have repented. But Jonah was like many of God's people when they sin. Instead of thinking clearly, he hardened his heart, kept his back turned to God, and plunged on into even greater alienation from Him.

The state of Jonah's heart is revealed clearly in his answer to the second question from the mariners: "What shall we do for thee, that the sea may be calm unto us?" Notice that it was not the mariners who thought up the idea of throwing Jonah overboard. They did not say, "What shall we do *to* thee?" They had said, "Tell us what to do to get out of this; we'll do anything you say."

And what did Jonah say? He might have called on them to repent of their sin and turn to Jehovah in order to become His followers. But Jonah was in the midst of sin himself, and so this answer was hardly open to him. Again, he might have tried to bluff his way out of the situation. He might have said, "I don't know what to do. God hasn't shown me. Here, give me an oar. I'll help you out." But Jonah could not say this either, for he knew what the consequences of such indifference would be. The storm would simply have gotten worse, and eventually everyone would have drowned. Finally, he could have said, "It is obvious what we must do. God wants me to go to Nineveh, and we will not be safe till I do. Turn the boat around. Let's go back. Then the storm will stop." I am sure that if Jonah had followed this course, not only would the storm have stopped but they would have had the best wind back to Joppa imaginable. But this is not what Jonah said either.

What did he say? The answer is a sad one. So determined was Jonah to resist the Lord's will that he actually said, "Take me up, and cast me forth into the sea; so shall the sea be calm for you; for I know that for my sake this great tempest is upon you" (v. 12). In other words, said Jonah, "I would rather die than do God's will."

Can a Christian become so hardened that he prefers death to what God wants him to do? It would be good if we could say no to that question, but unfortunately the answer is yes. By the grace of God it does not seem to happen too often, though it happens oftener than we might imagine. A Christian can become hardened. This is the course of sin. What begins easily with just a step to the west instead of to the east soon accelerates into a maelstrom of self-destruction.

An apparent illustration of this is the life of the late Bishop James Pike, who rose to national fame through his controversial opinions and frequent denials of church doctrines. At the beginning his denials were not very extreme. He denied the Virgin Birth (or at least questioned it) and presumably had a less-than-orthodox view of the Scriptures. But these wrong steps soon led to others. Thus, his ecclesiastical rise—he was the Episcopal bishop who in 1958, together with the Stated Clerk of the United Presbyterian Church, Eugene Carson Blake, launched the proposal for a gigantic merger of Protestant denominations later known as the Consultation on Church Union—was accompanied by an increasing decline of his commitment to other important doctrines. Even his own relatively liberal church was embarrassed, and there were several charges of heresy, though a heresy trial was avoided. There were also personal tragedies. Pike developed a drinking problem which led to his joining Alcoholics Anonymous. He had three marriages, the first being annulled and the second ending in divorce after producing four children. One son committed suicide. Pike drifted into the occult and claimed to have made contact with his deceased son through a Philadelphia medium named Arthur Ford. Finally, he left the church and at last died in 1969 in the Judean desert while researching a book on the historical Jesus; he reportedly told friends it would be the most sensational of his writings yet.

Pike's story is particularly tragic, both for his own sake and for those who were involved in his fate. But it is a pattern played out on a less dramatic level in the lives of many disobedient Christians. Disregard of God's Word or of others' fate (as Jonah of the fate of Nineveh) soon leads to a disregard of one's own. We must be warned and follow another path. Instead of brazening it out, we must learn to say with David, "Search me, O God, and know my heart; try me, and know my thoughts; and see if there be any wicked way in me, and lead me in the way everlasting" (Ps. 139:23-24).

True Conversions

Someone has said that non-Christians never look better than when they are compared with some Christians, and that is certainly true if the Christians are disobedient ones. It is true in this story. Jonah, in his disobedience, is quite willing that all the inhabitants of Nineveh perish; for his message is one of impending judgment, and his fear is that it might be suspended if he should preach to them and they should repent. But the mariners, themselves pagans like the people of Nineveh, are unwilling that Jonah (just one man) should perish even though he has brought them into a position of great danger. Jonah has said that he should be thrown overboard. The mariners have every right to heed him. But they are unwilling to see him die if it can be prevented. They do their best to save him. The Hebrew text says literally, "Nevertheless, the men *digged* to bring it to the land" (v. 13).

Even pagans have their limits, however. So at last, when it was evident that they could not win against the waves, they asked Jehovah to hold them guiltless for Jonah's death and then threw the rebellious prophet overboard. At once the sea ceased from its raging, and the men were left in silent wonder upon the gently rolling deck.

What happens next is the climax of chapter 1, in spite of the fact that the final verse tells of Jonah being swallowed by the great fish. That verse should really begin chapter two, and the verse that should end chapter one is verse 16. "Then the men feared the Lord exceedingly, and offered a sacrifice unto the Lord, and made vows." This verse means, quite simply, that the mariners were all saved through their experience with Jonah. It means that, in an ironic way, God was already accomplishing His purposes in spite of His prophet's stubborn rebellion.

The fact that the mariners were saved is evident in practically every word used. To begin with, this is the third time that the men are said to have feared something or somebody. The first was the storm (v. 5). The second was the disclosure that Jonah was a Hebrew who worshiped Jehovah (v. 10). This time they are said to have feared (that is, respected) Jehovah Himself. Obviously there is a progression.

Moreover, they were worshiping Jehovah. Earlier, when we are told of their prayers, we read: "Then the mariners were afraid, and cried every man unto his god," that is, to their idols. Now, after Jonah has been thrown overboard and the wind has stopped, we are told that they prayed to Jehovah, Jonah's God. And how did they worship precisely? Well, they performed sacrifices—this was the Jewish means of approach to God—and they made vows.

If the mariners had made their vows before their deliverance, I would not be so impressed. If they had made their vows first, theirs may have been only a foxhole conversion. We may imagine a situation in which a soldier is crouching in a foxhole looking down a hill against which an enemy is advancing. Naturally he is afraid for his life. So he begins to pray: "O God, if there is a God, don't let me get killed. I don't want to die. Save me! If You save me, I will do anything You want. I'll even...yes, I'll even become a missionary." He sees the soldiers advancing. But then suddenly they turn off in another direction. The battle shifts to the side, and he is saved. Does he remember his conversion? Not at all. He turns to his buddy and says, "Boy, we sure had a close call that time. Let's celebrate when we get leave next week. I know a place where we can drink and gamble and sin our fill." That is a foxhole conversion. This was what happened to Nelson Blount, founder of Steamtown U. S. A., who made several vows to God early in life but did not follow up on any of them till his wife was nearly killed in an automobile accident. But that is not what happened to the mariners. They made their vows after they had been delivered. Consequently, I believe that they were truly converted and that their vows must have been that they would serve Jehovah all their remaining days.

Irony and Great Grace

This incident is a great irony. We remember that Jonah was running from God because he did not want God to save the heathen in Nineveh. But the first great event in the story was the conversion of the heathen sailors, who were in many respects just like the pagans of Nineveh! And Jonah was not there to see it.

We must learn from this, for it carries us further in the lessons of this book about God's sovereignty. What God is going to do, God will do. If He has determined to save Mary Jones, God will save Mary Jones. If He has determined to save John Smith, God will save John Smith. Moreover, those whom He saves will never perish, neither will anyone pluck them out of Christ's hand (John 10:28). But notice, God can do this through the obedience of His children, as He does later with Nineveh through Jonah, in which case they share in the blessing. Or He can do it through His children's disobedience, as here, in which case they miss the blessing. Either way, God blesses those whom He will bless, but the one case involves happiness for His people while the other involves misery. Which will it be in your case? Will you resist Him? Will you refuse His Great Commission? Or will you obey Him in this and in all matters?

Perhaps you are not yet a Christian. If not, then you may learn from God's grace to the mariners.

You have not yet perished in your godless state because God, who made the sea around you and the dry land on which you walk, preserves you. Do not remain indifferent to Him. Turn to Him. Approach Him on the basis of the perfect sacrifice for sin made once by His own Son, Jesus Christ, and promise to follow Him throughout your days.

Chapter 3

Prayer
from the Depths

When Jonah was turning his back upon God, it did not bother him at all that God was thus abandoned by him. But suddenly, when Jonah was thrown overboard to his death, he found himself in the position of apparently being abandoned by God — which Jonah did not like at all. In the water and then in the great fish, he learned what hell was like, and it was there at the nadir of his misery that he repented and turned to God again.

Jonah was not really abandoned by God. But he felt that he was. It was in this last extremity that the hand of the Lord was, from our perspective, most evident. Ellul stated this clearly: "We should remember the significance of water in the Old Testament and then in the Church. Water denotes swallowing up and death. Yet it is also closely linked with the presence of the Spirit of God. This is part of the general principle that in God's revelation no sign is ever purely negative because God's own action is never negative. Most signs are ambivalent, and that which denotes death also has within it the promise of life. At the beginning of the creation story the waters symbolize the void, nothingness, the abyss. But we cannot stop there: the Spirit of God moves over the face of the waters" (*The Judgement of Jonah*, p. 41).

What Ellul says of the water is also true of the great fish with which this section begins. On the one hand, the fish was a symbol of total abandonment, of hell. Jonah even spoke of it in those terms. "I cried by reason of mine affliction unto the Lord, and He heard me; out of the belly of Sheol cried I, and Thou heardest my voice" (2:2). But on the other hand, it was (unknown to Jonah) the means by which God had planned to deliver him from the deep.

The Great Fish

It is almost a pity that the fish mentioned in Jonah has attracted so much attention; for in doing this it has detracted from the other very valuable lessons of this book. What has happened has been described well by Thomas John Carlisle, who wrote, "I was so obsessed with what was going on inside the whale that I missed seeing the drama inside Jonah." (*You! Jonah!*, Grand Rapids: Eerdmans, 1968, p. 21). Nevertheless, in being sensitive to the one danger we do not want to fall into the other danger of neglecting the miraculous nature of the story entirely.

So what of the great fish? Was it a whale? Did it really swallow Jonah? Can a person actually believe in such a story? Or is it so ludicrous as to make all refutation unnecessary?

One one level, a discussion of this problem is hardly necessary. Those who believe in the God of the Bible will have little difficulty ultimately in believing that such a miracle is possible. If the God of the Bible can raise up Jesus Christ from the dead,

He can certainly cause a great monster of the deep to be alongside a boat when His prophet is thrown overboard and can cause it to swallow him. On the other side, for those who disbelieve in miracles on principle, the evidence, whatever it may be, is meaningless. For if miracles do not happen, then this story about Jonah did not happen. It will not even help to point out that, strictly speaking, the swallowing of Jonah is not even a miracle, for to such minds the story will clearly be seen as a myth, not a fact.

On another level, however, a discussion of the miracle does have value. For instance, it shows that Christians who believe in such things are at least not totally unaware of the difficulties that may be involved. Or again, it may also show skeptics that the situation is not so unbelievable as they, perhaps without much thought or evidence, conceived that it was.

Britannica Research Service

It should be interesting to many skeptics that the Library Research Service of the *Encyclopedia Britannica* regularly distributes information supportive of the biblical narrative. This service is available to anyone who purchases a set of the *Encyclopedia*. Thus, anyone researching a subject and not finding that the *Encyclopedia* has covered it adequately, may write and ask for information on his subject, and a mimeographed report (generally pre-prepared) will be sent to him.

If a person requests information on the possibility of a whale having swallowed Jonah, a four-page report will be mailed, the bulk of which consists of information taken from an article on the "Sign of the Prophet Jonah and Its Modern Confirmations," which was published in the *Princeton Theological*

Review in 1927. It is followed by a bibliography in which some of the articles are supportive of the incident and some are not. The article itself concludes, "The story of Jonah occurs in Hebrew literature and tradition as an historical record. It can hardly be disputed that the tests applied to it are in fairness bound to be the most careful, accurate, and dispassionate that science and history can supply. Physiological tests entirely disprove the alleged impossibility of the story. It is shown by study of the structure of the sperm whale and its habits that it is perfectly possible for a man to be swallowed alive and after an interval vomited up again, also for him to remain alive for two or three days within the whale. Historical tests show that a similar event has happened in later times in at least one case, and that it is quite possible for an authentic record to have survived over even a much longer period than 700 years."[1]

The article leading up to this conclusion is in two parts. The first part distinguishes, as all honest writing on the subject has done, between those whales or other great fish that could conceivably swallow a man and those that could not. A generation ago one often heard that a whale could not swallow Jonah simply because the throat of the whale is too small. "A whale has difficulty swallowing an orange," was the viewpoint. This objection arose from a failure to distinguish between the Greenland whale, which does have a very small throat and which was the whale best known to seamen of an earlier generation, and the sperm whale or cachalot, which has an enormous mouth, throat, and stomach. An average specimen of the sperm whale might have

[1] A. J. Wilson, "Sign of the Prophet Jonah and Its Modern Confirmations," *Princeton Theological Review*, Oct., 1927, pp. 630-642.

a mouth 20 feet long, 15 feet high, and 9 feet wide; that is, the mouth would be larger than most rooms in an average-sized house.

It is known that the sperm whale feeds largely on squid, which are often much larger than a man. Whalers have sometimes found whole squid of this size in a dead whale's stomach.

As to whether a man could survive in a whale's stomach, the *Britannica* article maintains that he certainly could, though in circumstances of very great discomfort. There would be air to breathe, of a sort. It is needed to keep the animal afloat. But there would be great heat, about 104-108°F. Unpleasant contact with the animal's gastric juices might easily affect the skin, but the juices would not digest living matter; otherwise they would digest the walls of the creature's own stomach.

But has there ever been a case of a man actually having been swallowed by a whale and then regurgitated or saved by some means? This is the matter dealt with in the second half of the journal article, and apparently there are such cases. One case concerns a voyage of the whaling ship *Star of the East*, which in February, 1891 spotted a large sperm whale in the vicinity of the Falkland Islands. Two boats were launched, and in a short while one of the harpooners was able to spear the fish. Those in the second boat attempted to attach a second harpoon, but the boat capsized in the process and one man was drowned. A second sailor, James Bartley, disappeared and could not be found. In time the whale was killed and drawn to the side of the ship where it was made fast and the blubber removed. The next day the stomach was hoisted on deck. When it was opened, the missing sailor was found to be inside. He was unconscious but alive. Eventually he was revived by sea water and after a time resumed his duties on board the whaling vessel.

It is also possible, as the article shows, that the fish in question in Jonah's case may not even have been a whale. The Hebrew text merely says *dag*, which may be any kind of great fish. It may have been a species of shark, a Rhineodon or "Sea Dog," for instance; and if this is so, then there are other accounts of men being swallowed which are also relevant. The Sea Dog, while a member of the shark family, does not have the terrible teeth generally associated with sharks and grows to a size comparable to that of many whales. In his widely read book, *Kon-Tiki*, Thor Heyerdahl describes such a shark that followed his raft for a time in the mid-Pacific.

Jonah and Nineveh

In addition to the data on whales, there are also a number of ancient links between the prophet Jonah and Nineveh, which are also supportive of the Old Testament story. A few of these are cited by Gaebelein. First, there is a seal belonging to the reign of Amasis II of Egypt (570-526 B.C.), which shows with remarkable clarity a man emerging from a sea monster. This seal is cited by an archeologist named Knight in a volume entitled *Nile and the Jordan*, published in 1921. The figure had quite obviously been identified as Jonah. A second interesting bit of information is the name of the mound in the upper Tigris valley under which the remains of ancient Nineveh were discovered. The site of Nineveh had long been lost. But the mound had been called "Neby Yunas" ("The Prophet Jonah") for centuries.

Gaebelein then points out that the association of Jonah and his story with ancient Nineveh may have been preserved due to the worship of the fish-god

Dagon which went on there. Normally the experiences of Jonah before his preaching in Nineveh would have had little effect on the preaching itself or on the response in Nineveh. But if Jonah had been swallowed by a great fish and had then been thrown up on the coast of Phoenicia, perhaps in the sight of witnesses who may have conveyed this tale to those of Nineveh, it is easy to see how a population that worshiped a fish-god may have received him readily as a divine messenger and have remembered and preserved the tale long afterward. Whatever the case, the association of Jonah with Nineveh seems to be an old one.

A Turning Point

To concentrate so much upon what happened inside the great fish that we miss noting what happened inside Jonah is to make a great mistake, however, as I have indicated. So we must now turn to Jonah's prayer to God from inside the monster. As we read it we discover that the prayer reveals the truly great miracle. It shows that though Jonah had been brought to the depths of misery within the fish, he nevertheless found in his misery the mercy of God. He discovered that though he had forsaken God, God nevertheless had not forsaken him, even though it seemed that He had. In brief, Jonah found salvation within the fish even before it had thrown him up on the land.

With the exception of verse 10, the second chapter is entirely a record of this prayer. Since the book is only four chapters long it is obvious that the prayer is important, "Then Jonah prayed unto the Lord, his God, out of the fish's belly, and said, 'I cried by reason of mine affliction unto the Lord, and He heard me; out of the belly of Sheol cried I, and Thou heardest my voice. For Thou hadst cast me into the deep, in the midst of the seas, and the floods compassed me about; all Thy billows and Thy waves passed over me. Then I said I am cast out of Thy sight; Yet I will look again toward Thine holy temple. The waters compassed me about, even to the soul; the depth closed me round about, the weeds were wrapped about my head. I went down to the bottoms of the mountains; the earth, with its bars, was about me forever; yet hast Thou brought up my life from corruption, O Lord, my God. When my soul fainted within me, I remembered the Lord; and my prayer came in unto Thee, into Thine holy temple. They that observe lying vanities forsake their own mercy. But I will sacrifice unto Thee with the voice of thanksgiving; I will pay that that I have vowed. Salvation is of the Lord'" (2:1-9).

Four Principles

Jonah's prayer has four major characteristics of all true prayer. Further, we notice that these characteristics should be in our own prayers at all times, particularly when we get into trouble because of disobedience and need to repent and get ourselves back on the right path.

The first is *honesty*. The prayer is starkly honest. So often Christians are dishonest in their prayers. They come to the Lord trying to overlook some circumstance that He has caused, ignore some sin that He has highlighted, or obtain some request that He has already clearly rejected.

What we do may be illustrated by a story frequently told by the late Donald Grey Barnhouse. On one occasion his daughter had come to him with a request which he had denied. "Well, then, what do you want me to do?" she asked. He told her what he wanted and then went on with his work. She remained standing in front of him.

At length Mrs. Barnhouse called to the daughter from another room. "Where are you? What are you doing?" she asked.

The daughter replied, "I am waiting for Daddy to tell me what he wants me to do."

At this point Barnhouse lifted his head and said to her, "Whatever you are doing, you are not waiting to find out what I want you to do. I have told you what I want you to do, but you do not like it. You are actually waiting to see if you can get me to change my mind."

Any perceptive Christian can see himself in that story, for many of our prayers are only attempts to get God to change His mind to let us do something He has already clearly forbidden. Moreover, if at that point we go on to reject His will and thus reap the fruits of our disobedience, we frequently try to explain away the results.

Christians ought to be the greatest realists in the world. But they are not, especially when they are disobeying God or running away from Him. Instead of being honest about their trouble, as Jonah was, they find themselves trying to explain their miseries away. They say, "Well, I suppose that things like this just happen." Or, "It's hard, but I can handle it; maybe if I just keep going, things will get better." Jonah did not do this. Instead, in verses 3-6 he acknowledged his trouble—he had been cast into the deep, the floods had covered him, he was cast out of the sight of God (from all appearances), he had gone down to the bottoms of the mountains of the earth, and, barring a miracle, the earth was about him forever.

Jonah not only acknowledged his misery; he acknowledged that it was God who had caused it. "Thou has cast me into the deep," he said. Not circumstances! Not the mariners! It was *"Thy* billows," *"Thy* waves." We might argue that the mariners did have a role and that it was Jonah himself who had suggested that he be thrown overboard. But these are minor technicalities, and Jonah is done with technicalities. These do not matter. He was in desperate straits, and God was the One who was doing it.

In one sense, this increased the terror of his situations. The situation was bad enough. He was far from land with no path of escape. But add to this the fact that God had allowed it to happen. God had addressed Himself to Jonah in the character of a judge, He had summoned him to trial, witnessed against him, cast a verdict of guilty, and then sentenced him to death, proceeding at once to the implementation of the sentence—this was a terror almost beyond words. Hugh Martin, who notes this, observes, "Oh! if he found courage or composure amidst circumstances like these to address his soul in prayer, and that, too, believing prayer, to the Lord, how great a marvel or miracle of grace must that prayer be!" (*The Prophet Jonah*, p. 193).

On the other hand, there is also a sense in which the acknowledgement of God's presence, even in judgment, is a great comfort. For it is better to fall into the hands of God, even in judgment, than to be apart from Him.

David is a case in point. At the very end of 2 Samuel we are told that David sinned in causing the people of Israel to be numbered and that God, through the prophet Gad, gave David three choices, one of which was to be God's judgment. David could choose seven years of famine, three months of defeat before his enemies, or three days of pestilence in the land. David chose the latter because, he said, "Let us fall, now, into the hand of the Lord; for His mercies are great. And let me not fall into the hand of man" (2 Sam. 24:14). It was a wise decision; for though the judgment came, we read that when the plague reached Jerusalem "the Lord repented of the evil, and said to the angel who destroyed the people, 'It is enough; stay now thine hand'" (v. 16). Our God is a God of judgment, but His judgment is tempered by that mercy which is so prominent a theme in Jonah.

Penance

The prayer of Jonah is also characterized by a deep spirit of *penance*. Penance is an old-fashioned word, but it is a good one. It means "confession, self-abasement, or mortification showing sorrow of and repentance of sin." Clearly, this is a step beyond mere honesty, for it is possible to be honest about one's situation and even acknowledge that God has caused it and yet be unrepentant about it. We can acknowledge that God caused it but then get angry.

In one such instance a Christian girl insisted on marrying a man who was not a Christian, ignoring the advice of her pastor and friends, and then knew great misery as the marriage turned sour and ended in divorce. She knew that the situation was her own fault and that the breakup of the marriage was only an inevitable outworking of God's laws in her own particular situation. But she resented God for it. Thus, instead of repenting of the sin, she drifted away from Christian friends and activities. Only much later, by the grace of God, did she return to Him.

We know that Jonah's was a prayer of true penance in two ways. First, he acknowledged that everything that had happened to him, while caused by God, was nevertheless his own fault. He deserved it.

This is the meaning of verse 8, one of the great verses of the book: "They that observe lying vanities forsake their own mercy." A "lying vanity" is an idol, therefore anything that takes the place of God. One's "own mercy" is the measure of mercy which God normally shows to His children. So what Jonah is saying is that whenever a believer puts something else in the place of God and thereby turns from Him, he inevitably also turns from that mercy which God constantly shows him. God is not less merciful, but the believer has rejected that mercy and therefore deserves all that comes upon him.

Jonah's prayer showed true repentance also in that Jonah did not ask God for anything. If he had, we might suspect that his repentance had a hidden motive. We might think that he was repenting just to get God back on his side, so he could get out of the fish and back on dry land. But he asked for nothing. He was genuinely sorry for his disobedience.

Thanksgiving

The third characteristic of Jonah's prayer was *thanksgiving*, a puzzling fact. "Thanksgiving?" we might ask. "Why thanksgiving? What could Jonah, swallowed by a fish and in the midst of the ocean awaiting death, possibly have to be thankful about?" If we continue to ask the question in terms of a physical deliverance, there is no answer; Jonah's attitude continues to be puzzling. But if we ask the question in spiritual terms and think of a spiritual deliverance, the answer is easy. True, Jonah had no hope of deliverance from the fish. But he had found the grace of God again—his own word is "salvation" (v. 9)—and for this he was profoundly thankful.

Jonah was not thankful that God had delivered him, because God had not yet delivered him. He was not thankful that God was going to deliver him, because he had no idea that God was going to do it. What he was thankful for was that God had turned him from his rebellion and had caused him to call once again upon the name of the Lord. He was thankful for salvation. He was thankful for the continuing and abiding grace of God.

Ellul discusses the prayer in these words: "Jonah has not been answered if we take the answer to be rescue from the belly of the fish, salvation from hell. But he has been answered if we take the answer to be adoption under the care of the God who takes on the totality of our sufferings, dramas and situations. He is answered because grace does not fail in any way, and even if there is no visible, actual and personal sign, Jonah can state that the answer takes place because grace has been granted to him from all eternity. Jonah rediscovers this grace of God at the very moment his situation is hopeless and to all appearances nothing more is to be expected. His refusal and flight were clearly outside grace. Events have taken place without any indication of a favorable intervention, only signs of judgment. But suddenly, when he has accepted his condemnation, when he has acknowledged before God that he was guilty and that God was just, he sees that at no point did God cease to show him grace . . . .

"Nothing proves this to Jonah. No fact confirms his insight. He does not have even the first beginning of deliverance. But simply in the very fact that he has been able to repent, to condemn himself, to recognize the sentence of the just judge, he has reason enough to say: 'Thou hast delivered me.' It is here indeed that the great decision is taken" *(The Judgement of Jonah,* pp. 48-49).

It is also here that the great miracles are performed.

It is not when history is redirected by some super-natural, spectacular event, not when bodies are brought to life or heavenly bodies are stopped in their normal motion that the great miracles occur. It is when a human heart comes to acknowledge its own personal sin and confess it before God and when, as a consequence, God restores the broken Creator—creature relationship.

Sacrifices and Vows

There is one final characteristic of Jonah's prayer that should not escape notice; for, in terms of his own rebellion, it is the most significant of all. It is that *Jonah is now ready to take his place alongside the ungodly.* Earlier he had said, "I am a Jew, and I do not want to preach to heathen." Now he was willing to take a place beside them as one who needed God's mercy and who had indeed found it.

A person may ask, "But where do you find that in the story?" You find it in an obvious parallel between verse 9 of this chapter and verse 16 of chapter 1. Verse 9 says, "But I will sacrifice unto Thee with the voice of thanksgiving; I will pay that that I have vowed." The earlier verse says, speaking of the mariners, "Then the men feared the Lord exceedingly, and offered a sacrifice unto the Lord, and made vows." The mariners, who were heathens, learned to approach the Lord as He must be approached—through the blood of an innocent victim sacrificed for their sin and through a personal commitment expressed in a vow. Jonah, the prophet of the Lord, also approached through the sacrifice (promising to do in the future what he obviously could not do in the belly of the great fish, if that should ever be possible) and made a vow.

It is hard to miss the point. Jonah, despite his

earlier protestations, came to God, not as a Jew who deserved special privileges or concessions, but as a sinful human being who was one with all other sinful human beings and who needed God's grace.

It is thus with us all. If you come to God claiming privileges, boasting of your own special achievements and therefore expecting God to accept you or acknowledge you on the basis of your own merit, you have not a hope of salvation. Indeed, the Scriptures say explicitly that God will not pay court to human merit: "For by grace are ye saved through faith; and that not of yourselves, it is the gift of God — not of works, lest any man should boast" (Eph. 2:8-9). But if, on the other hand, you will come to God, admitting that you deserve nothing from Him but His just wrath and condemnation, if you will place your faith in His Son, the Lord Jesus Christ, who willingly became your sacrifice, and if you will promise to serve Him as His faithful disciple till your life's end, then He will save you and you will enter into a deep experience of the abiding grace of God, as did Jonah.

Charles W. Colson, known nationally because of his involvement in the Watergate scandal, is one who recently found this kind of grace. By his own confession, Colson had been driven by pride, as many of us are. But he came to see this one night in the living room of a good friend, Thomas Phillips, president of the Raytheon Company, who had just become a Christian. As they talked, Phillips shared the story of his own conversion and then read from the chapter in *Mere Christianity* in which C. S. Lewis speaks of pride being "the chief cause of misery in every nation and every family since the world began." This struck Colson forcefully, and he acknowledged (privately) that it was true of him. A few minutes later, after he had left the Phillips' home and was seated in his own car, a tremendous sense of release came over him and he prayed, crying, "God, I don't know how to find You, but I'm going to try! I'm not much the way I am now, but somehow I want to give myself to You. Take me.[1] At that point Colson had not yet understood the importance of the death of Jesus Christ, and he had certainly not surrendered his life to Him. But the prayer was honest and repentant. Colson was coming to God as a sinner. And the God who receives sinners (and only sinners) heard him and rapidly led him into a full knowledge of Christ and the assurance of salvation.

No one has ever truly repented till he or she has come to acknowledge that there is nothing in any person that can possibly commend him or her to God. And no one has ever been saved who has not come to God on the basis of the sacrifice which He alone has graciously provided.

The very last phrase of the prayer makes this quite plain: "Salvation is of the Lord" (v. 9). Salvation is possible only because God makes it possible. It is all of Him.

Jesus Saviour

"Salvation is of the Lord!" This thought was a blessing to Jonah; but if it was a comfort to him, it should be even more of a comfort to us who live this side of the Cross of Jesus Christ. For this is what "Jesus" means. When the angel explained the meaning of the name to Joseph he said, "Thou shalt call His name Jesus [Jehovah saves]; for He shall save His people from their sins" (Matt. 1:21). The wording is slightly different, of course; but the

---

[1]Charles W. Colson, *Born Again* (Old Tappan, N.J.: Chosen Books/Fleming H. Revell, 1976), pp. 108-117.

meaning is precisely the same: "Salvation is of the Lord!"

Thus far in our study of Jonah we have stressed that the story of this rebellious prophet is our story. But we should not miss the point that in another sense it is also the story of our Lord, who went down to hell for us bearing our sin and then was raised from the dead to bring many sons with Him into glory. In other words, Jonah is a story of salvation, and this story is always God's story. Have you seen that truth? A marginal note in the New Scofield Reference Bible indicates the sentence "Salvation is of the Lord" (v. 9) is "the theme of the Bible," and indeed it is. We have run from God, all of us. But none need perish. God has Himself provided the way into eternal life through the death and resurrection of His beloved Son.

Chapter 4

The Greatest Revival in History

The third chapter of Jonah contains the high point of this remarkable story. For, however remarkable the preceding action has been and however great the miracles, the most remarkable action and the greatest miracles are in the results of Jonah's preaching to the Ninevites. The result was the greatest and most thorough revival that has ever taken place. Writes Gaebelein, "Heretofore the emphasis has been upon the prophet's preparation; tremendous as the miracle of Jonah's preservation in the sea monster has been, it is more of a preface than a conclusion. Now the veil is drawn aside, and something of the strange purpose of the Almighty in dealing with His prophet is revealed. If the miracle of the fish is great, that of this chapter is greater. For here is the record of nothing less than the greatest mass conversion in history. Though generalities must always be used with caution, we may say that never again has the world seen anything quite like the result of Jonah's preaching in Nineveh" (*Four Minor Prophets*, p. 95).

The first noteworthy fact about this great revival

is that it began with God's call to just one man — Jonah. And even that was after he had apparently disqualified himself from future service.

The Second Time

We cannot really imagine what it would be like if we were in the place of God, nor should we. But if we were God and if we were confronted with the situation as we have found it at the end of chapter 2, I imagine that at this point we would say that we had had just about enough of Jonah. We would recall that Jonah was a man whom we had chosen to be a prophet and to whom we had imparted a special measure of understanding in spiritual things. We would remember that we had already given him a full and blessed ministry in Israel and that we had then called him to do a tremendous work in Nineveh. Jonah should have been delighted. But instead of being delighted, he had refused this call. Finally, he had become so set in his determination that he had declared that he would rather die than return to the place of blessing. He had requested to be thrown overboard. Moreover, we would recall that even then we had been gracious to him. Instead of allowing him to die we had saved him. We had brought him to a place of repentance. Then we had spoken to the fish, and it had returned Jonah to the land.

How gracious we had been! No one could expect more. So if we were God and if we should reason at this point that we had saved Jonah but that he had nevertheless disqualified himself from ever being a prophet again, who could blame us? If we were to say, " Go home now, Jonah. I am glad you have repented of your disobedience, but you are no longer useful to me," we would be just and reasonable in so doing. But this is not God's way. Thus, instead of reading of

God's rejection of Jonah, we find these words: "And the word of the Lord came unto Jonah the second time, saying, 'Arise go unto Nineveh, that great city, and preach unto it the preaching that I bid thee'" (V. 1-2). The important point is that God came to Jonah the second time and that the commission was the same as on the first occasion.

Is God like that? Does God stoop to use those who have rejected His calling, turned a deaf ear to His word, and pursued a course of determined disobedience? Yes, He is like that. Yes, He does use such messengers. If He did not, none of us could serve.

We find the principle of the Lord coming to an individual a second time quite often in Scripture. Take the case of Abraham, as an example. The word of the Lord came to Abraham when he was still a devil worshiper living in Mesopotamia, like all his family. The fact that they were a family of idol, and therefore devil, worshipers is stated in several Old Testament passages (Josh. 24:2-3, 14; Isa. 51: 1-2). The story of Rachel's having hidden the idols of her father (Gen. 31) shows that Abraham's relatives still owned and cherished idols at least three generations after God had called him out of Mesopotamia. But God called him out of Ur of the Chaldees and sent him around the northern edge of the great Arabian desert to Palestine, which God was giving him. Stephen recalls this word in his speech saying, "The God of glory appeared unto our father, Abraham, when he was in Mesopotamia, before he dwelt in Haran, and said unto him, 'Get thee out of thy country, and from thy kindred, and come into the land which I shall show thee'" (Acts 7:2-3). We might think that such a revelation and promise would undoubtedly have caused Abraham to travel all the way to the land God was giving. But when we read the account (Gen.

11 — 12) we find that he did not. Abraham left Ur, it is true. But he stopped at Haran which was still hundreds of miles from Palestine. Undoubtedly he would have stayed there were it not that God came to him the second time. God said on this occasion, "Get thee out of thy country, and from thy kindred, and from thy father's house, unto a land that I will show thee; and I will make of thee a great nation, and I will bless thee, and make thy name great; and thou shalt be a blessing" (Gen. 12:1-2).

The same is true of Moses, who became under God one of the great national leaders of all history. We are not told much detail of the early life of Moses, only that he was raised by his mother with the blessing of the daughter of Pharaoh for the first months or years of life and that he was afterward raised in the palace of the Pharaoh. Still we know that God had revealed Himself to Moses during this period, for in the same speech of Stephen that mentions Abraham, we read that when Moses killed the Egyptian he did so supposing that "his brethren would have understood how that God by his hand would deliver them" (Acts 7:25). This was Moses' way of bringing about a deliverance, but it was not God's. Consequently, Moses had to flee from Egypt to Midian, where he lived for the next 40 years. We might say that Moses had ruined his chances and destroyed his future ministry. Yet after he had lived in Midian for this long period of time and when he was 80 years old, God appeared to him in a burning bush, saying, "Come now, therefore, and I will send thee unto Pharaoh, that thou mayest bring forth My people, the children of Israel, out of Egypt" (Ex. 3:10). God had appeared to Moses a second time.

We turn to the New Testament and find the same thing to be true in the case of the Apostle Peter.

Peter had boasted that no matter what should happen he would not desert the Lord. "I am ready to go with Thee, both into prison, and to death," Peter had said. But Jesus revealed that Peter would deny Him three times before morning. And Peter did (Luke 22:33-34, 54-62). What shall be done with Peter now? Shall he be cast off? Shall he be disqualified from future service? We find that the Lord appears to Peter to recommission him to service, asking on three separate occasions (corresponding to Peter's three denials), "Simon, son of Jonah, lovest thou Me?"(John 21:15-17). When Peter answers on each occasion, "Yea, Lord, Thou knowest that I love Thee," Jesus responds, "Feed My sheep." The Lord came to Peter a second time.

A number of years ago a young girl in Philadelphia felt the call of God to Christian service. But she married a non-Christian, who shortly thereafter left her to go his own way. The experience brought the girl back to desiring God's will. But what was she to do? Should she divorce him? The Scriptures clearly taught that she should not follow this course, for according to 1 Corinthians 7, she was to be open to any possible reconciliation. She decided rightly to leave the matter entirely in God's hands. Thus, after having confessed her sin to God, she let her separated husband know that she was open to reconciliation if he desired it. When he declined, she let the matter rest. Within a few months her husband was suddenly killed in a car accident, and God directed her to apply to Wycliffe Bible Translators for missionary work. The word of the Lord clearly came to her a second time, and she is now serving as a translator in South America.

And the Lord comes again to all of us who are His true children. Have we never, like Abraham, stopped at our Harans? Of course, we have. We are sent on errands, and we never get there because some sin or some preoccupation detains us. Have we never, like Moses, taken matters into our own hands and formulated our own plans? Of course, we have. And we have even denied our Lord on occasions when we should have spoken for Him. We have disobeyed Him. We have run away from Him; and some of us, like Jonah, have run very far away indeed. Does God cast us off? Does He disown us? No! He disciplines us, it is true. But having done that and having brought us to the place of repentance and surrender, He returns the second time to recommission us to service. Moreover, He comes a third and a fourth and a hundredth and a thousandth time, if necessary, as it often is. None of us would be where we are now in our Christian lives if God had not dealt thus with us. O the greatness of the unmerited grace of our God! We deserve nothing. Yet we receive everything, even when we foolishly reject it and turn from it.

William Banks, in *Jonah, The Reluctant Prophet* (Chicago: Moody Press, 1966, p. 72), speaks of such grace particularly as it comes to Christian people today. "We are moved to speak of Jonah's God as the God of the Second Chance. But honest sober reflection compels the saint to speak of Him as the God of the 999th chance! Such gracious mercy as was extended to Jonah here, and to David, and to the dying thief upon the cross, and to Peter—surely it has been granted to all believers through the precious blood of Jesus Christ."

Two More Lessons

Two more important lessons appear from this passage. The first comes from the fact that when the word of the Lord came to Jonah the second time, it came with the same commission that he had received the first time.

We often think, when we are on the verge of running away from God, that if we run away and if the Lord should nevertheless speak to us again, He might take note of the fact that we have run away and therefore change the command, but He does not. When we think or act in this disobedient way, we are acting like children who do not like what they are being told to do and who therefore throw a tantrum, thinking that this might get the parents to change their minds. An indulgent or foolish parent might fall for this attempt at manipulation, but a wise parent does not. Nor does God! Consequently, after He has dealt with the tantrum, sometimes by means of a spanking, God returns to us with the same commission He gave before. So why try to resist it? Instead, learn that if you try to run away from God, He sooner or later is going to catch up with you and that, when He does, you are going to have to face the very thing you are running away from. Learn to experience His grace now instead of His Judgment.

The second lesson is found in the one change in this second expression of the commission. You will remember that the first commission had three key verbs in it: arise, go, and cry. In this commission the first two verbs are the same. But the second phrase, "Cry against it," is changed to "Preach unto it the preaching that I bid thee." When we remember that the greatest revival in world history followed Jonah's doing precisely that, we may well reason that the spiritual life of our own time would be quite different if that commission were only followed by those thousands of clergymen who fill our pulpits each Sunday. They preach. No one doubts that. But are their words the words which God has given them?

Is their preaching that which He has bid them proclaim? Today God's ministers are called to proclaim the message of the Bible, embodying all the counsel of God. But many consider this unsophisticated or old-fashioned and so substitute the words and supposed wisdom of men. Thus, their words lack power and bring judgment upon their own heads.

Obedient at Last

The first time the word of the Lord came to Jonah telling him to go to Nineveh, Jonah ran away. This time, having learned the consequences of running away, Jonah obeyed. Note the wonderful contrast to the similar command recorded in chapter 1. In that chapter, after God had told Jonah, "Arise, go to Nineveh, that great city, and cry against it," we are introduced to the prophet's disobedience through the words, "*but* Jonah, . . ." Here, after the identical commission, we read, "So Jonah arose, and went into Nineveh, according to the word of the Lord" (v. 3). This is something we might well covet for every true Christian. Too often we try to out-guess or out-maneuver God. We try to "out-but" Him. Our reply to God should not be "but"; it should be "so." Did God say it? Then let us do it. Let it be said of us, "So John Smith, Mary Jones (or whatever your name may be) arose and went according to the word of the Lord."

And what will be the result? In the first chapter, after Jonah had voiced his "but" to God, he soon found that God had an even greater "but" to say to him. Jonah's "but" involved his running away. God's "but" involved the storm, the salvation of the mariners, the preparation of the great fish, the repentance of Jonah, and at the last a new commission to Nineveh. On this occasion Jonah's conduct is introduced by the word "so." What follows? "*So* the people of Nineveh believed God, and proclaimed a fast, and put on sackcloth, from the greatest of them even to the least of them" (v. 5). In other words, Jonah's "so" was followed by an even greater "so" on the part of God.

What made the difference? Simply that Jonah was now walking "according to the word of the Lord." In the first instance, he was trying to get away from that word. In the second instance, the word was with him. The author of Hebrews says rightly, "For the Word of God is living, and powerful, and sharper than any two-edged sword, piercing even to the dividing asunder of soul and spirit, and of the joints and marrow, and is a discerner of the thoughts and intents of the heart" (Heb. 4:12). It is through His word alone that God brings blessing and opens the closed and rebellious hearts of men.

A Great Revival

When Jonah finally entered Nineveh he began to proclaim his message: "Yet forty days, and Nineveh shall be overthrown" (3:4). That does not seem to be a very impressive message. In the English Bible it is only eight words, and in the Hebrew it is even shorter—five, *Hod arbahim yom wenineveh nehpaketh.* The words are a simple prophecy of judgment. Yet they were greatly blessed, because they were truly God's words and not the words of a mere man. According to the following verses they were used of God to bring about a genuine and pervasive revival in the city.

We can almost see Jonah as he entered a day's journey into the city and began to cry out his message. What would be his reception? Would the Ninevites laugh? Would they turn against Jonah and persecute him? As he cried out people stopped to listen. The hum of commerce died down and a holy hush stole over the collecting multitudes. Soon there were weeping and other signs of a genuine repentance of sin. At last the message of Jonah entered even the palace, and the king, divesting himself of his magnificent robes, took the place of a mourner alongside his repenting subjects. We read, "For word came unto the king of Nineveh, and he arose from his throne, and he laid his robe from him, and covered himself with sackcloth, and sat in ashes. And he caused it to be proclaimed and published through Nineveh by the decree of the king and his nobles, saying, 'Let neither man nor beast, herd nor flock, taste anything; let them not feed, nor drink water. But let man and beast be covered with sackcloth, and cry mightily unto God; yea, let them turn every one from his evil way, and from the violence that is in their hands. Who can tell if God will turn and repent, and turn away from His fierce anger, that we perish not?' " (vv. 6-9)

What did the people believe? Whom did they believe? We are not told that the people believed Jonah, in spite of his deliverance and the fact that the Lord Jesus Christ later declared that Jonah was in some sense himself a "sign" to the Ninevites (Luke 11:30). What we are told is that "the people . . . believed God." Faith should never rest in the messenger, but rather in God, who gives the message. This is one mark of all true revival and true preaching.

Scholars have sometimes objected to taking the account of the revival literally on grounds that the information furnished about the city is not accurate. For example, it has been pointed out that though the city was indeed large—the circumference of the inner walls was about seven and three-fourth miles—

it is hardly possible, even with extremely crowded streets, that it would have taken Jonah three days to cross it. But the answer to this is that the description "an exceedingly great city of three days' journey" probably refers to what we would call the fullest extent of the city including the suburbs. It may even refer to a fuller, geographical area including farms and outlying fortifications. A parallel to this comes from the cities of the Middle Ages. In Europe during the Middle Ages, people lived near walled cities in order to be able to retreat into them when danger threatened. But in times of peace, when no danger threatened, people often spilled beyond the walls to farm and carry on other occupations. This was true of hundreds and thousands of cities, even little ones. It would obviously be true of a large capital city such as Nineveh.

The city was genuinely large and the revival miraculous, as all true revivals are. It is therefore somewhat breathtaking to come to the true high point of the story in the account of God's repentance from bringing judgment and read, "And God saw their works, that they turned from their evil way; and God repented of the evil that He had said that He would do unto them, and He did it not" (v. 10).

The Repentance of God

That this and other verses in the Bible speak of God "repenting" or changing His mind has been a problem for some students of Scripture. But it should not be, once the phrase is understood.

To begin with, its usage is obviously a case of employing human language to describe that which is ultimately beyond human language. God is always beyond our understanding. Consequently, we should not be surprised when phrases like this tend to confuse us. We should simply balance them with other statements, like that of Balaam, who said, "God is not a man, that He should lie; neither the son of man, that He should repent. Hath He said, and shall He not do it? Or hath He spoken, and shall He not make it good?" (Num. 23:19) If we must choose between apparent contradictions, obviously we must side with the truth that God is not changeable and that He does not deal falsely in the revelation of Himself to men.

Second, we must realize that in this case there is not even a true contradiction. For the city that God had promised to destroy, the wicked city of Nineveh, ceased to exist after Jonah's preaching. True, it came back, as Nineveh slipped into sin again years later. We find Nahum writing explicitly of a judgment that did indeed eventually come. But for now the city ceased to exist as sinful Nineveh and therefore came to enjoy God's blessing. Here Martin writes perceptively, "It was wicked, violent, unrighteous, atheistical, proud, and luxurious Nineveh which God had threatened to destroy. A city sitting in sackcloth and ashes, humbled in the depths of self-abasement, and appealing as lowly suppliants to His commiseration—a Nineveh like that—*that* Nineveh, He had never threatened. *That* Nineveh He visited not with ruin. He had never said He would. The Nineveh which God threatened to destroy passed away; it became totally another city—far more so, in virtue of this change in moral state, than if it had been translated from its olden geographical position, and wholly transformed in its architectural appearance. Surely its great moral change had made it more truly another place—a kind of new creature, old things having passed away, and all things become new—than any alteration in its physical aspect could have done. It really, in God's estimation, is not the Nineveh He threatened at all. The terrific threatening does not apply now. 'God saw their works';—their fruits meet for repentance, namely, that they turned from their evil way;—and God repented of the evil that He said that He would do unto them, and He did it not'" *(The Prophet Jonah,* pp. 290-291).

Ultimately, however, the problem posed by the repentance of God is solved, not by observing the repentance of men and women, but by noticing that God repents of the evil that He would do by taking the punishment for that evil upon Himself. The Hebrew word for "repent" used of God is most often *nacham,* which speaks of an inner suffering needing to be consoled. Did God suffer? Not at the time of Jonah and the Ninevites, of course. But He did so later in the person of His Son, the Lord Jesus Christ. in Jesus God took all the world's evil upon Himself precisely so that He might repent of the necessity to visit the out-working of that evil upon men. Ellul is one who saw this clearly. He wrote, "In reality God's repenting in the face of man's repentance is Jesus Christ. Each time there is any question of this repenting in Scripture we thus have a new prophecy of Jesus Christ who puts into effect both the justice of God and also the love of God without doing despite to either the one or the other" *(The Judgement of Jonah,* p. 100).

Here the message of Jonah hits quite close to home. Like Jonah and the Ninevites, each of us today needs to repent of sin and turn to the righteous and merciful God of the universe. But our repentance from sin, assuming we do repent, is made possible only because God Himself first repented of the evil by taking our judgment upon Himself. Jesus bore our judgment. Consequently, our turning from sin must be at the same time a turning to Jesus through whom alone we have forgiveness.

Steps to Revival

The repentance of the Ninevites suggests the steps we should follow if we have not come to that kind of repentance. It suggests "four distinct steps" to a revival of true godliness and religion, as Gaebelein indicates in his perceptive study.

First, there must be a *faithful preaching* and a *faithful hearing* of the Word of God. Jonah preached what God had given him to preach, and it was highly effective. It was not a lengthy message, but that did not matter. It was not an intellectual message either, but that did not matter. Perhaps it was not even an eloquent message, but neither did that matter. All that was necessary was that it was God's message, preached and heard in the power of God's Holy Spirit.

Charles Haddon Spurgeon, one of the greatest preachers who ever lived, was saved by such a message. He was a boy at the time, and he had gone to a Primitive Methodist Chapel whose pulpit was filled on that particular morning by a man who had no education and could barely read or write. He preached on the text, "Look unto Me, and be ye saved." He stuck to it, for he had little else to say.

"My dear friends, this is a very simple text indeed. It says, 'Look.' Now lookin' don't take a deal of pain. It ain't liftin' your foot or your finger; it is just, 'Look.' Well, a man needn't go to college to learn to look. You may be the biggest fool, and yet you can look. A man needn't be worth a thousand a year to be able to look. Anyone can look; even a child can look. But then the text says, 'Look unto *Me*.' Ay, many of ye are lookin' to yourselves, but it's no use lookin' there. You'll never find any comfort in yourselves.... Look to *Christ*. The text says, 'Look unto *Me*.'" After about 10 minutes of such preaching the speaker had quite exhausted what he had to say. But he noticed the young Spurgeon sitting under the balcony and, fixing his eyes on him, went on, "Young man, you look very miserable. And you always will be miserable—miserable in life, and miserable in death—if you don't obey my text; but if you obey now, this moment, you will be saved. Young man, look to Jesus Christ. Look! Look! Look!" It was not a polished sermon. But it was a true sermon based on God's Word, and God blessed it. For Spurgeon did look and was converted.[1]

How much we need this preaching today! There is no greater need in America or in any other part of the world today than hearing the clear preaching of the timeless truths of the Word of God and a clear reception of them by those who are, or are in the process of becoming, God's children. If we would have blessing in our personal lives, it must come about by a response to the teachings of this Book. If we would have blessing in our churches and in our land, the same response is necessary. So flock to any faithful preaching of God's Word, and fill your mind with it. If you are in a position to share it with others, do so clearly and without apology. Do not mind that unbelievers scoff. Do not mind that liberal scholars pronounce it untrue. God will send blessing.

Second, there must be *belief in God*. Notice that the Ninevites did more than just hear Jonah's message. As soon as the Ninevites heard they responded. This is the way it has always been and must be.

---

[1] Spurgeon tells this story in his *Autobiography, Volume 1: The Early Years, 1834-1859* (Carlisle, Pa.: The Banner of Truth Trust, 1973), pp. 87-88.

There is no other way in which men and women come to believe in God; but having heard the Word many do come to Him. People are not led to faith through visions. Give a person a vision of God, and he will declare it interesting. But it will not lead him to faith. "Faith cometh by hearing," says the Bible, "and hearing by the Word of God" (Rom. 10:17).

Third, having heard the word of God and having believed God, the city then took *action* upon its faith by proclaiming a fast and putting on the clothes of mourning. There is no true belief without some corresponding action. For example, in the Book of Hebrews, in that great chapter on faith (chapter 11), we are told that Abel believed God and *offered* a proper sacrifice, Enoch *pleased* God, Noah *prepared an ark,* Abraham *obeyed* and *went out* from his own home to a new land that God would show him, Isaac *blessed Jacob* according to God's instructions, Jacob *blessed* the sons of Joseph, Joseph *gave commandment* for his body to be brought back to Canaan at the time of the Exodus, Moses *refused* to be called the son of the Pharaoh's daughter but *chose rather to suffer affliction with the people of God than to enjoy the pleasures of sin for a season.* In each case belief resulted in specific action by which the person's trust in God was demonstrated.

In the 19th century there was a well-known acrobat (Jean Francois Gravelet) who was known by the stage name Blondin because of his fair coloring. Blondin had gained a reputation for himself in Europe before coming to America, but once here he gained even greater fame by walking across Niagara Falls on a tightrope. Thereafter he was associated in everyone's mind with the Falls. He did numerous stunts on his crossings. On one occasion he pushed a wheelbarrow across. On another he paused to eat an omelet. Once or twice he carried his manager on his back. On one of these latter occasions, after he had reached the edge once again, he is said to have turned to a man in the crowd and to have asked him, "Do you believe I could do that with you?"

"Of course," answered the man. "I've just seen you do it."

"Well, then, hop on," invited the acrobat. "I'll carry you across."

"Not on your life," replied the spectator.

Clearly there was a form of belief in the man's first response, but it was not the kind of belief that results in action. What is called for spiritually is a belief that will fully commit itself to Jesus, thereby allowing Him to carry the believing one over the troubled waters of this life.

Thomas Skinner, one of the most effective black evangelists in America, once demonstrated the reality of his new belief in Christ by immediately informing the members of his New York City street gang of his conversion, even though he knew that it would be interpreted as a sign of weakness and that some would welcome the opportunity to turn on him.

Finally, as part of this action, there must be a *turning from specific sin*. The Ninevites turned from the sin that was most characteristic of them — violence. We read in verse 8, "Let them turn every one ... from the violence that is in their hands." We too must turn from our specific sins whether sexual indulgence, pride, selfishness, lack of love for our Christian brothers and sisters, laziness, materialism, or whatever it may be. We must not repent in general terms only. We must repent specifically, if we would be blessed by God and come to know Him more fully.

Chapter 5

God More Merciful Than His Prophet

I doubt if there ever has been a story of God's dealings with men that should give more cause for rejoicing than the story of Jonah. Jonah's story is a story of God's mercy. First, there had been mercy for Jonah, who had been given a great commission. Even though he rebelled at the idea of preaching to the pagans of Nineveh, God persevered with him to turn him from his folly and bring him at last to that great capital city of Assyria. God's mercy to Jonah involved the storm, the great fish, the repentance of Jonah within the fish, and then God's recommissioning of Jonah after he had again been cast up on the shore. We read at that point that "the word of the Lord came unto Jonah the second time, saying, 'Arise, go unto Nineveh, that great city, and preach unto it the preaching that I bid thee'" (3:1-2).

Parallel to the story of God's dealing with Jonah is God's dealing with the mariners who were manning the ship that was taking Jonah to Tarshish. This too shows God's mercy. The mariners were pagans at the beginning of the story. We are told that in the midst of the storm "every man cried unto his [own] god" (1:5). But by the end, after they had heard Jonah's testimony and had witnessed the calming of the sea after the rebellious prophet had been thrown overboard, we find them all worshiping Jehovah, offering sacrifices and making vows.

Finally and greatest of all, there is the account of God's mercy to Nineveh. Nineveh was not a godly city. On the contrary, it was a particularly wicked city. But God used the preaching of Jonah to bring about a revival in Nineveh, probably the greatest revival in history. We read that "the people of Nineveh believed God, and proclaimed a fast, and put on sackcloth, from the greatest of them even to the least of them" (3:5). The repentance was so great that even the king was affected. God postponed the judgment that Jonah had prophesied.

If there had ever been a cause for rejoicing, certainly those three evidences of God's mercy—first to His prophet, then to the mariners, and eventually to Nineveh—should provide it, and we should expect Jonah himself to be literally leaping with joy and thanksgiving. Instead, when we come to the fourth and final chapter, we find Jonah in the worst "blue funk" imaginable. In fact, he was angry about it, violently angry. And, of course, he was angry with God.

We find a series of additional lessons in this chapter as God dealt with Jonah at the depth of his own attitudes. In these final encounters the book more or less comes full circle. At the beginning it was the story of just two personalities—Jonah and God. After Jonah had run away, the mariners came into the story and then eventually all the people of Nineveh. Now at the end we are back to God and His rebellious prophet again.

It is always that way. God gives us work to do; the work involves other people. But in the end, when it gets right down to basics, it is always a question of each of us as an individual and God. It is a question of whether or not we have obeyed Him.

Jonah's Displeasure

Jonah's anger at God's mercy to the people of Nineveh is disclosed in the first three verses of chapter 4, so it is to these that we must turn for an analysis of Jonah's mood. The verses say, "But it displeased Jonah exceedingly, and he was very angry. And he prayed unto the Lord, and said, 'I pray Thee, O Lord, was not this my saying, when I was yet in my country? Therefore, I fled before unto Tarshish; for I knew that Thou art a gracious God, and merciful, slow to anger, and of great kindness, and repentest Thee of the evil. Therefore now, O Lord, take, I beseech Thee, my life from me; for it is better for me to die than to live" (4:1-3).

Obviously, Jonah is angry. He had obeyed God, doing what God wanted; but God had not done what Jonah wanted. Jonah had said that judgment was coming in 40 days, but it had not come. He felt betrayed. He felt that God had let him down by not destroying the city as he, Jonah, had predicted. Moreover, in all this he had not the slightest interest in the people of Nineveh, for he should have been happy at their deliverance. Instead, he was displeased that God had not wiped them off the face of the earth and sent them to hell forever. If God had destroyed the city, he would have returned home delighted.

In Jonah's anger at God we notice three significant things. First, he tried to *justify himself* both in his own eyes and in the eyes of God. That is, he tried to justify his former disobedience. He said, in effect,

"This is the reason I refused to go to Nineveh when You first called me, and, what is more, I was right in refusing."

One Friday night when I was in seminary, I was invited by a former headmaster of the Stony Brook School on Long Island to come up to the school that weekend to preach in the Sunday morning chapel service. Normally, I would have been delighted with such an invitation. But this was a Friday night of exam week, and I had an important examination on Monday morning. In those days I did not have a collection of sermons I could fall back on. So I knew that if I accepted this invitation, I would have to spend most of Saturday preparing my sermon. Then I would have to drive up to the school on Saturday evening, and on Sunday afternoon and evening I would have to drive back. I knew that I would come to the examination on Monday morning with virtually no time having been spent in study. Well, I explained this to my former headmaster, but he was very persuasive. Moreover, he said that if I put the Lord's work first, the Lord would take care of the exam. I remember thinking that He probably would *not* take care of it, as least to my satisfaction. But I thought I should take the assignment anyway; so I went. And sure enough, I did not get the A on the exam that I had been expecting; I got a B-. At that point I found myself on the verge of saying to God, "You see, God, I shouldn't have done what You requested because it turned out exactly as I predicted." Fortunately, however, God gave me wisdom to know that in this case the difference between one grade and another was next to nothing but that the preaching was important.

The point of this illustration is that we all do what Jonah did. Things do not turn out as we wish, so we seek to justify our disobedience before God. What we need to learn is that we are not sufficient to pass on the appropriateness or inappropriateness of the outcome, nor are we responsible for it. We are responsible only for performing the whole will of God.

The second thing that Jonah did in his anger is somewhat harder to explain, but it is still easy to notice. Jonah tried to *turn God against God.* Or to put the same thing in other language, he tried to quote God's word back to Him in his warped desire to show that he, Jonah, was right and that God was wrong. This is what he was doing in verse 2, for he was probably thinking of Exodus 34:6-7 as he argued. The verses in Exodus say, "And the Lord passed by before [Moses], and proclaimed, The Lord, the Lord God, merciful and gracious, long-suffering, and abundant in goodness and truth, keeping mercy for thousands, forgiving iniquity and transgression and sin.". "Now," said Jonah, "is that or is that not what You have said? And if it is what You have said, why did You send me to Nineveh with a message that You never intended to fulfill? Is it not true that I, Jonah, am the consistent one and that You are two-faced and wrong?"

Each reader of the book should find this frightening. It is frightening in itself and also frightening because of its parallels. What is the most infamous of all attempts to turn the word of God against God? It is Satan's attempt to quote Scripture in his temptation of the Lord Jesus Christ. Jesus had replied to Satan's first temptation to turn stones into bread by quoting from Deuteronomy 8:3: "It is written, Man shall not live by bread alone, but by every word that proceedeth out of the mouth of God" (Matt. 4:4). But Satan immediately retaliated by quoting some Scripture of his own. He took Jesus to a pinnacle of the temple and challenged Him to throw Himself over, saying, "It is written, He shall give His angels charge concerning Thee, and in their hands they shall bear Thee up, lest at any time Thou dash Thy foot against a stone" (Matt. 4:6). It was a quotation of Psalm 91:11-12, but he used it wrongly as Jesus next pointed out. Jesus replied that it is not possible to use one verse of Scripture to overthrow another, and the Bible clearly says, "Thou shalt not put the Lord, thy God, to the test" (Matt. 4:7; Deut. 6:16).

Satan was using the Bible, the very Word of God, to justify evil and show that the course God had set for Himself was not right. This was what Jonah was doing. So at no point is the diabolical nature of his rebellion more evident than here. In seeking to justify himself and prove God wrong by Scripture Jonah took his place as Satan's own spiritual progeny.

Jacques Ellul applied this to our own tendencies to self-justification. "This is a great warning; it is not enough to lean on a biblical text to be right; it is not enough to adduce biblical arguments, whether theological or pietistic, to be in tune with God. All this may denote opposition to God. It may even be a way of disobeying Him. The using of God's word to tempt God is a danger which threatens all Christians. Every time the Christian thinks he has God's word in store to be used as needed, he commits this sin, which is that of Satan himself against Christ. This is the attitude of the historian who dissects Scripture to set is against Scripture, of the theologian who uses a text to construct his doctrine or philosophy, or of the simple Christian who opens his Bible to find himself justified there, or to find arguments against non-Christians or against Christians who do not hold the same views, arguments which show how far superior my position is to that of others. It is not for nothing the Bible shows us that this attitude of Jonah is that of Satan . . . This should stir us to great caution in the reading and use of the Bible. It is not a neutral book which one can read and then take arguments from it. It is an explosive power which must be handled with care" *(The Judgement of Jonah,* p. 74).

This of course, does not mean that we should leave the Bible alone and not study it. We avoid the danger Ellul speaks of by faithfully applying this formula: When we find ourselves reading the Bible to find verses and passages that justify our own behavior, we are wrong and are in danger; on the other hand, when we read Scripture and find verses that expose our sin and thereby draw us increasingly close to God who will forgive us our sin and cleanse us of all unrighteousness, then we are on the right track and will find blessing.

Ellul said, "What revelation teaches us about ourselves is all to the effect that we are not righteous, that we have no means of justifying ourselves, that we have no possibility of disputing with God, that we have no right to condemn others and be in the right against them, and that in this extreme distress only a gracious act of God which is external to us (though it becomes internal) can save us. This is what Scripture teaches us, and if we stick to this, reading the Bible is useful and healthy and brings forth fruit in us" (p. 75).

Jonah did one more thing in his anger, and at that point it was almost comic: *he asked for death again.* "Therefore now, O Lord, take, I beseech Thee, my life from me; for it is better for me to die than to live" (v. 3). It is hard to understand the prophet's apparent death wish. When he had run from God and God had caught up to him in the storm, he thought it would be better to die than obey. So he asked the mariners to throw him overboard. Now, having obeyed, he is still unhappy and says once more that he would rather die and get it all over. It is a warning that it is possible to obey God but to do so with such a degree of unwillingness and anger that so far as we are concerned, the obedience is no better than disobedience.

What Is Wrong, Jonah?

At this point of the story we rightly ask ourselves, "But what is wrong with Jonah?" He should have been happy, but he was unhappy. He had been instrumental in the gift of spiritual life to thousands, but he preferred death. He claimed to be cognizant of God's grace and mercy, which he himself had experienced, but he resented God for it and said that he would really have preferred wrath and justice for Nineveh.

First, we cannot help noting that one thing wrong with Jonah is that he is not reconciled to the will of God, even yet. He had been opposed to God's will at the beginning and had run away because of his opposition. God had pursued him and had brought him to the point of obedience. He had even experienced the marvels of a rediscovery of God's grace while in the belly of the great fish and had repented of his sin with one of the most moving and genuine prayers of repentance in all Scripture. Perhaps only David's great psalm of repentance can be said to rival it (Ps. 51). And yet, in spite of all this, Jonah's attitudes had not really changed. He was still unwilling to see the people of Nineveh saved, and he resented the God of mercy for having saved them. He had not yet truly reconciled himself to the will of God.

We often act the same, even when we are apparently obeying God. We are doing what we think we should be doing, living the kind of life we think a Christian should live. But secretly we are unhappy and angry with God for making the requirement. For this reason many Christians look and act miserable much of the time.

Second, Jonah had forgotten God's mercy to him. We object, "But how could Jonah of all people forget God's mercy? And forget it so quickly?" Jonah was the one who should rightly have perished miserably inside the great fish. He had renounced God. It would have been only proper if God had renounced him. Yet God had showed him great mercy, first in bringing him to repentance and then in saving him and recommissioning him to preach in Nineveh.

Jonah had certainly experienced mercy at the hand of God. But there was the long journey across the desert, and man's memory is short. Jonah simply forgot how gracious God had been to him. He had forgotten God's mercy and therefore was ill-prepared to appreciate it when God showed the same mercy to other men and women. We must remember this whenever we find ourselves wondering, somewhat regretfully, why God does not judge someone else for his sin. When we do that—as we all do—we are forgetting that we were once where that other person is now and that we would not be where we are now were it not for God's great mercy to us.

The third reason why Jonah was angry was that he did not know God as well as he thought he did. Undoubtedly, he was proud of his knowledge of God. He was a Jew, first of all, and the Jews had received an accurate revelation of God which the pagans did not possess; they had the Law and the record of God's dealings with men in history. Moreover, Jonah was a prophet—not just any Jew, but rather one who had studied the Law and who had been commissioned by God and given special revelations by Him. If anybody knew God, it was Jonah! But did he? He knew something of God, it is true. But he did not know God well enough to grieve over sin as God grieves over sin, or to rejoice at the repentance of the sinner. Instead, he was like the older son of Christ's parable, who sulked while the father celebrated, and felt cheated by the prodigal's good fortune.

We need to apply that to certain ways of thinking in our day. For example, we sometimes find ourselves wishing that the Lord Jesus Christ would return, usher in the final judgment, and escort His own into heaven. We are grieved when unbelievers scorn our belief in the Second Coming. We wish He would come. We cannot understand Christ's delay. But this is because we do not understand God well enough. Peter knew people who thought like this, and he wrote an explanation to them saying, "There shall come in the last days scoffers, walking after their own lusts, and saying, 'Where is the promise of His coming? For since the fathers fell asleep, all things continue as they were from the beginning of creation'...But, beloved, be not ignorant of this one thing, that one day is with the Lord as a thousand years, and a thousand years as one day. The Lord is not slack concerning His promise, as some men count slackness, but is long-suffering toward us, not willing that any should perish, but that all should come to repentance" (2 Pet. 3:3-4, 8-9).

Peter explained the delay of God's judgment by reference to God's mercy, saying that Jesus has not yet returned in order that all whom God desires to call to faith in Him might be born, have the Gospel preached to them, and believe. Are you not glad that Jesus did not return before you were born and believed in Him? Well then, rejoice that His delay makes possible the salvation of countless others. God is a God of judgment. But He is also a God of mercy. We need to know Him as that.

Three Questions

Jonah had not learned this, however. So God began to teach him more about His mercy, doing so by means of three significant questions which conclude the book.

God likes to ask questions because they are effective in helping sinful human beings see the state of their own hearts. God asked questions of Adam and Eve. He asked, "Where art thou?... Who told thee that thou wast naked? Hast thou eaten of the tree, whereof I commanded thee that thou shouldest not eat?... What is this that thou hast done?" (Gen. 3:9, 11, 13). He directed a question to Cain after he had murdered his brother: "Where is Abel, thy brother?... What hast thou done?" (Gen. 4:9-10). Saul was asked the same thing after he had foolishly intruded into the priest's office by offering the sacrifices: "What hast thou done?" (1 Sam. 13:11). After David had sinned in committing adultery with Bath-sheba and having her husband killed, Nathan came to him to ask, "Why hast thou despised the commandment of the Lord, to do evil in His sight?" (2 Sam. 12:9). God asked Isaiah, "Whom shall I send, and who will go for Us?" (Isa. 6:8). Jesus asked Judas, "Friend, why art thou come?" (Matt. 26:50). "Betrayest thou the Son of man with a kiss?" (Luke 22:48) It is the same in the Book of Jonah, for God asks, "Doest thou well to be angry?... Doest thou well to be angry for the

gourd? .. Should not I spare Nineveh, that great
city, in which are more than sixscore thousand
persons that cannot discern between their right
hand and their left hand; and also much cattle?"
(vv. 5, 9, 11).

What does God's first question to his sulking
prophet mean: "Doest thou well to be angry?"
Quite simply it is a challenge to Jonah to judge
whether the angry prophet or the great and holy God
of the universe is right. It is as though God had said,
"We are looking at the identical situation in two
different ways, Jonah. I am pleased with it. You are
angry. Which of us has the proper perspective?"
Whenever God asks us that type of question, we
must recognize that whatever our thoughts or feelings
may be, it is always God who is correct and not we.
"Let God be true, but every man a liar" (Rom. 3:4).

Jonah did not think like that. He did not confess
his error. Instead, he got even angrier and left the
city. On its outskirts he constructed a little shelter
for himself, and then waited to see if God might not
destroy the city after all. Suddenly God's promise to
destroy Nineveh seemed very important to him.

Here he made three great errors, as Ellul points
out. First, *he quit.* He abandoned his mission to
Nineveh even though he had no right or instruction
by God to do it. If God had sent Jonah to Nineveh
to preach to them and if then as a result of Jonah's
preaching the people had repented and turned to
Jehovah, Jonah should have stayed and taught them
more perfectly, becoming a Calvin to Nineveh just
as the great Protestant reformer was blessed to the
city of Geneva. But Jonah was not willing to do this
and so left the city. In the same way, many Christians
today abandon the work that God has given them,
because God does not carry through according to

their expectations or their timetable. Thus, students abandon their work when it begins to prove difficult. Parents sometimes give up on their children. Many abandon their jobs. Ministers sometimes quit the ministry when the results are not all they anticipate or when the going gets rough. We have no right to do that.

Second, Jonah built *a little shelter for himself,* a private retreat, which again he had no right to do. Were there no shelters in Nineveh? No homes? No place where the prophet of Israel, who had been the vehicle of such great spiritual blessing, would be welcome? Of course, there were. But Jonah was not interested in these shelters, because he still secretly despised the people of Nineveh and hoped that God would judge them. To put it starkly, Jonah launched a little separatist movement in which he established his own independent church or denomination—all because he disliked the people of Nineveh. Ellul wrote, "He creates his own domain in the shade where he will be at peace according to his own measure, just as Christians try to make a church according to their own measure—it is not the body of Christ—and a divine kingdom according to their own measure, full of intentions which are good and effective and well-constructed, but which are only a fresh demonstration of their autonomy in relation to God" (*The Judgement of Jonah,* p. 79).

Jonah's third error was to become a *spectator,* for we are told that he sat in the shadow of his booth "till he might see what would become of the city" (v. 5). He was not called to be a spectator, any more than Christians are called to be spectators of the world's ills and misfortunes today. He was called to identify with those people and help them as best he could by the grace of God.

Something for Jonah

Jonah had still not come around to God's way of thinking, but God had not given up on him. God had a second question. But before He asked it, He did something to prepare Jonah's heart for the message. First He caused an unusually fast-growing plant, a gourd, to spring up next to Jonah's rude shelter. We are told that it became a shadow for him, that is, a protection from the blazing desert sun. We read, "So Jonah was exceedingly glad of the gourd" (v. 6).

That is remarkable—that Jonah was "exceedingly glad." For it is the first time in the story that Jonah had been glad for anything. The first thing that we read about in the story was God's commission to him to preach in Nineveh, but he had not liked that. Then there was the storm, and he had not liked that. He did not like the great fish, even though it had been the means of saving him from certain death. Apparently, he had not been happy even with the second commission, when the word of the Lord came to him a second time. He obviously had not been happy with the repentance of Nineveh. Nothing pleased him. But here at last "Jonah was exceedingly glad." Why? The answer is obvious. Jonah was pleased because at last, after all the compassion of God for other people, God was finally doing something for Jonah. Selfish? Of course, it was. And petty too! For the gourd was a trifle compared with the conversion of the entire city of Nineveh.

Having caused the gourd to spring up, God then did something else. He caused a worm to attack the root so that the plant withered. And after that He caused a vehement east wind to blow off the desert, which brought Jonah to the point of fainting from the terrible heat. Jonah was angrier than ever, and again he expressed a desire to die.

At this point God asked His second question. His first question had been, "Doest thou well to be angry?" It was a question as to who was right—God or Jonah. This time God asked, "Doest thou well to be angry for the gourd?" By this question God exposed Jonah's pettiness, for his anger had brought him from the grandeur of being angry at God—One who is at least a worthy opponent—to be angry at a petty thing as a plant or worm.

The same thing happens when we become angry. We begin by being angry at big things, but very quickly we become angry at petty things. First we are angry with God. Next we express our anger at circumstances, then minor circumstances. Finally, our shoelace breaks one morning, and we find ourselves swearing. God was showing him this, saying in effect, "Look where your anger has taken you, Jonah. Is this right? Is this the way to live? Do you want to spend the rest of your life swearing at petty annoyances?"

At last God asked His final question, and it is with this question that the book closes. God asked, "Should not I spare Nineveh, that great city, in which are more than sixscore thousand persons that cannot discern between their right hand and their left hand; and also much cattle?" Jonah had been sorry for the plant. So God does not talk to him about the adult population of the city, who undoubtedly deserved the judgment that Jonah was so anxious to have fall upon them. God talks about the cattle, who were innocent, and the smallest children, designated as those who could not yet discern between their right hand and their left. Was God not right to show mercy for their sake, if not for the adult population? Does not even Jonah's compassion for the gourd vindicate God's judgment?

Wideness in God's Mercy

The book ends with a question, a question which has no written answer. This is not a mistake. It ends on a question in order that we and each one who reads it might ask himself the same question. Is God not right? Is He not great for showing mercy?

The lessons of this book are many. There are lessons that concern Jonah himself. He is a type of practically everything: a type of Christ (who was buried but who rose again); a type of Israel, a type of all believers (for we all run away from God at times and need to be disciplined). There are lessons that concern Nineveh and the true meaning of repentance. There are lessons relating to the doctrine of God's sovereignty over men and nature.

But greater than all these lessons is the lesson of the greatness of the mercy of God. How great is God's mercy? We have a hymn which says, "There's a wideness in God's mercy like the wideness of the sea." But even that is not wide enough. The real measure of the wideness of the mercy of God is that of the outstretched arms of the Lord Jesus Christ as He hung upon the Cross to die for our salvation. That is the wideness of God's mercy. That is the measure of the length to which the love of God will go.

How can we, who have known that mercy and benefited from it, be less than merciful to others? How can we do less than love them and carry the Gospel to them with all the strength at our disposal?